THE ART OF

HOME

LANDSCAPING

PUBLISHED BY **F. W. DODGE CORPORATION,**

NEW YORK

Printed and bound in U.S.A.

Library of Congress Catalog Card Number: 56-8103

TO **PEACE AND PROSPERITY**

FOREWORD

Like any other artist, the landscape architect needs an appreciative and understanding audience. A co-operative relationship between artist and audience is most productive of good results for both. The primary social function of the landscape architect is his ability to put together all the complex and disconnected elements of outdoor development into recognizable units of useful and pleasant landscape space. No other technical competence has any meaning in landscape design without this ability.

This book is intended to distill for you as completely as possible the knowledge and understanding which I have developed through twenty-two years of training and experience. I have attempted to accomplish this in clear and straightforward language. If I fall at times into words or phrases that are too abstruse, it is because I am a landscape architect, not an expert in the art of writing. I have included certain ideas not generally found in "how to do it" books, because they are essential to your understanding of the problem.

If this book gives you understanding and appreciation of the importance of this unifying design process, the effort of writing it will have been richly rewarded.

Although this book bears my name as author, it is not a one-man product. All of the work illustrated — unless otherwise credited — is the product of Eckbo, Royston, and Williams, a landscape architectural firm of four partners, six associates, and two offices, in Los Angeles and San Francisco. All of the graphic illustrations, as well as their general layout and design, are the work of Carlos Diniz, an artist whose talents are equalled only by his enthusiasm for doing a good job in excess of the requirements. Typographic and jacket design are by Peter Oldenburg. Many thanks are due to the many correspondents across the country who responded with so much care to my queries about regional planting. Although this proved too big a project for inclusion in this book, the carton of material which is accumulated is carefully stored for future reference.

Los Angeles
October, 1955

CONTENTS

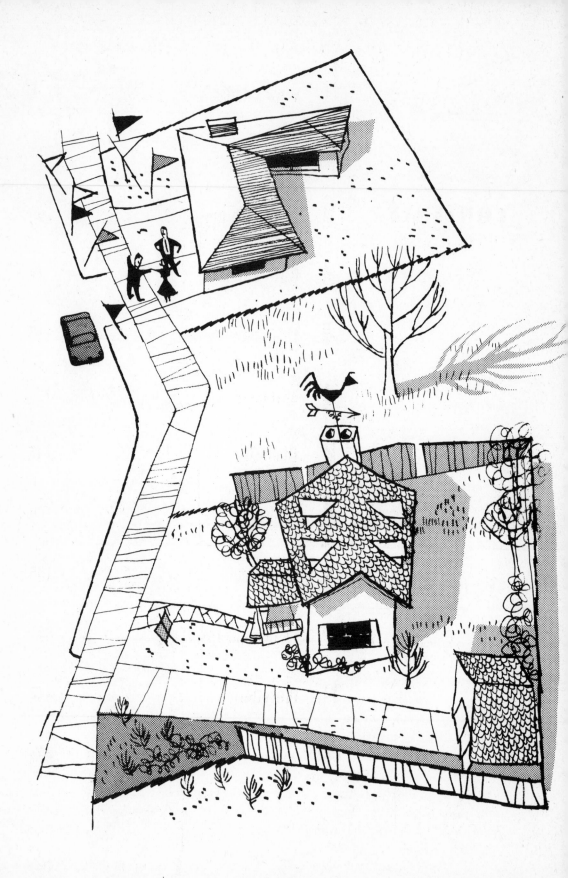

1. Why Landscape?

The purpose of this book is to help you solve the typical, average, common home-planning problems that appear in the outdoors around all of our houses. Perhaps while reading the chapters that follow you will discover that your property, whether old or new, has more possibilities than you had realized.

Let's begin with a fable:

Once upon a time two vacant houses and one empty lot sat quietly staring at the street in front of them. The street was in Suburbtown; neither rich nor poor; not very old and yet not new; quite middle. One house had just recently been built and was for sale. The unplanted yard was full of realtors' and open-house signs and colored flags. The other house was old enough to be looking a little run-down. It had a few overgrown shrubs around the foundations, and a 4-ft. board fence around the back yard. It too was for sale, but there was only one realtor's sign in its yard. The empty lot was between the two houses. It was empty of everything but weeds, beer cans, and one rather dilapidated elm tree in the center.

On Sundays a good many families drove around the streets of Suburbtown looking for houses. A couple of new factories had recently opened nearby, and the town was expanding. It wasn't long before the vacant new house was bought by a family named Newfield. It was quite attractive: one-story ranch style with the living room opening through to the back. They moved in just as soon as they could, even before the escrow closed. The older house was not especially attractive: two stories high, with a big front porch, living room across the front, kitchen and laundry to the rear. A month or two later it was bought by a family named Overbee.

1

The Newfields moved in on a Saturday. By Monday morning they were fairly well settled, and by Tuesday night Mrs. Newfield was beginning to complain about dust and dirt from the unplanted yard. At breakfast on Saturday Mr. Newfield said he guessed they had better get started on the landscaping. Every week end for some time after that there was great activity around their house. Grass was planted front and back, and miscellaneous shrubs and trees were collected from friends and relatives, and a few bought at the local nursery. These were planted around the house and in the grass, with much discussion and guesswork as to what they might do. Mr. Newfield and two friends built a 5-ft. concrete block wall around the backyard in two week ends and three cases of beer. On the following week end he laid a 10-ft. flagstone terrace across the rear living-room opening, dusted his hands, and settled down to the television that evening with the pleasant sense of having completed a good job.

In the meantime the Overbee family had moved into the old house two lots away and had begun to take stock of their new home. It wasn't the modern space-for-living that they had dreamed of; but the price was right and they had to get settled. They had a large collection of clippings from house-and-garden magazines, many books on house and garden planning, and they had spent many long evenings poring over them and projecting a dream home. Now they sat across the dining table, thumbing through all this literature and glancing at the house around them, and at the garden seen through the windows.

"Henry," said Mrs. Overbee, "here we are, moved into a real house with our collection of dreams and ideas. How on earth are we going to make them come true here? This doesn't look anything like any of our pictures."

"Well, Martha," said Henry, "it does seem awfully complicated. The trouble is that the houses in all of these stories are planned to open on the gardens and show interest in them—kind of like our neighbor two doors down. But this house turns its back on the garden—the back yard is a total loss."

"But there are lots of ideas in these clippings for making nice, modern, free-form gardens—and I've saved some beautiful color schemes. Can't we just fix up the back yard into a nice patio, repaint the living room and dining room, and try to enjoy this place?" Martha sounded a bit wistful.

Henry answered very carefully: "Honey, I know you're tired of the gypsy life we've been leading. You just want to settle down and relax for a while. But I don't want to go off half-cocked. We've made that mistake before. A patio is no good if we can't get to it. You notice how busy the people in that nice new house two doors down have been—all their landscaping is done already. But it's a mess—they'll be doing it over again in six months.

Doesn't look as though they thought seriously once while they were doing it. Just slapped everything in, and practically spoiled that nice new house."

"I know, Henry. Isn't it too bad! Well, what do you think we should do?"

"I must admit I'm a little stymied as to how to translate all this beautiful living in pictures into reality in this house and lot. I don't know how to put all these things together."

"Henry, I've got an idea. You remember how, when we got ready to buy a house, we sat down and took inventory of our finances and resources— to see what we could afford? And how we decided we had to find a place in a certain price bracket, in the right location for your work, my shopping, and the kids' school? We made a plan and followed it. That's what we should do here."

"I suppose you're right. I *guess* I could draw one. . . ."

"First we have to take inventory, make a survey of what we have here. Then we have to make a list of everything we want, as specifically as we can. Let's do that first and see how it looks."

So they bought some graph paper in large sheets ruled both ways at eight squares to the inch. They bought a small drawing board and some thumb tacks and a 50-ft. tape. And they spent the next Saturday measuring up their property and plotting it on the graph paper.

It was fun. First they measured all around the house, from corner to corner. They plotted as they measured, and when they returned to the first corner they found themselves two squares away on the paper. It took them fifteen minutes to discover that they had skipped over a jog in the chimney. When they had corrected this they measured from each corner in two directions in line with the walls, to the side and rear property lines (as they appeared to be defined on the ground by fences and planting) and to the sidewalk in front. While doing this they marked, as accurately as possible, locations for their few shrubs and trees, and for the walks and back fence. Then, at Henry's insistence, they went back around the house and located all the doors and windows, and their heights above the ground. The house floor was 2 ft. off the ground in front, but only a foot in back.

They pondered this at lunch. "The house couldn't have settled that much," said Henry.

"Then the ground must slope. And we thought we had a flat lot!" said Martha. After lunch they borrowed a hand level from an acquaintance across the street, and learned how to read the levels at different points in the yard by holding a marked stick vertically. They found that their lot sloped 3 ft. up from front to back, plus another foot in the 10 ft. next to the sidewalk. They began to feel like full-fledged surveyors.

"Guess that's everything," said Henry.

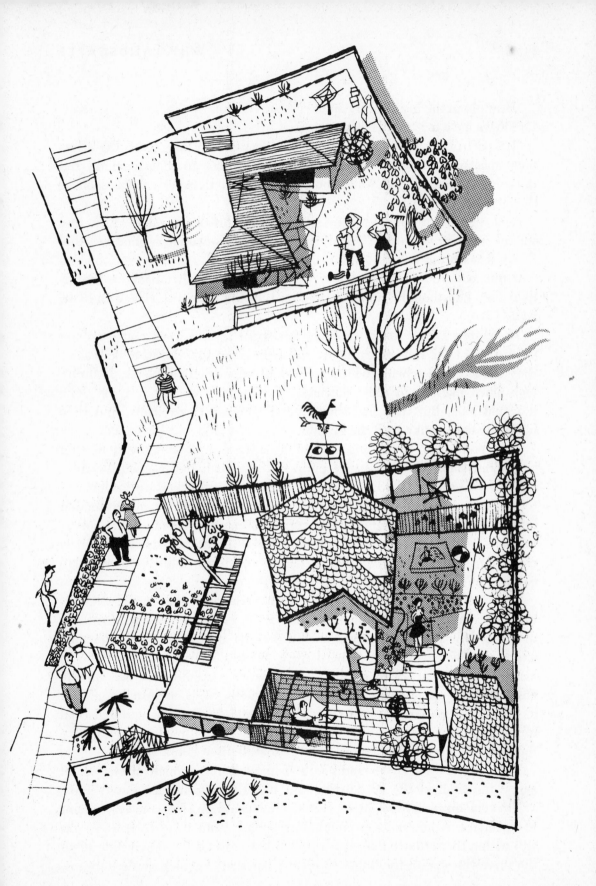

"How about the inside of the house?" said Martha.

"Do we have to?" said Henry wearily.

"It's part of our problem," said Martha firmly. And they spent the afternoon measuring the downstairs rooms, and trying to plot them on the drawing so that all the walls showed the same thickness. That evening they relaxed at a movie.

Next morning (Sunday) they cleared the breakfast table early and spread out their plot plan. "Say, this is a real bird's-eye view," said Martha, "but is it really our lot?"

It did look different. The house was quite a bit farther back on the lot than they had thought, and the side yard on the driveway side was 15 ft. wide.

To shorten a long story, the Overbees spent several week ends working out a plan. Four rolls of cheap tracing paper and two dozen pencils later they arrived at a scheme which seemed to solve their problems. It didn't look much like any of their clippings; in fact, they weren't sure just how it would look. But they had thought it through very carefully, and they felt ready to carry it out on the ground.

They had begun by writing a program, a list of everything they needed or wanted. This included a nice patio for outdoor living in good weather; a sheltered entry for bad weather; clothes lines and other work elements together in one part of the yard; shade in summer and wind protection in winter; a cut-flower bed; a messy corner for son John, and a quiet corner for daughter Imogene; a workshop for Father's occasional spurts of handicraft, and outdoor storage for a variety of tools and pieces of play equipment.

They made endless little diagrams of the right sizes, shapes and descriptions for these various elements, and they made endless patterns for dividing their yard space up in such a way as to fit in all these elements and make them work. It was hard work, because it was hard for them to visualize just what all these shapes and patterns would look like on the ground. They spent many hours outdoors with sticks and string, trying to project the patterns at full size. Their final scheme, still in rough plan form, didn't look slick or professional, but it looked as though it would solve their problems and give them maximum use from their house and lot.

They found that by extending their front porch (which stretched all across the front of the house) to about twice its width, they could make a very good-sized outdoor living space. This would be close and convenient to the living room, and yet could be screened from the street, as it was still within the set-back line. It was possible to extend the porch roof along the driveway side of the house to form a car shelter which made unnecessary the tortuous drive to the rear garage. By adding a new door in this end of the living room, and a new brick walk between driveway and house, a new sheltered entry was provided. This made it possible to screen the new front patio entirely from the front walk and drive, as well as from the street. A new dimension could be added to the house, and waste space rescued from an over-large front yard.

The rear yard, no longer cluttered with the family car, was divided into thirds, one for daughter, one for son, one for work space and cut-flowers. This left the old garage to be converted to workshop and storage. Tall evergreen boundary planting was projected to cut out the hot western sun and the cold north wind. All this, of course, still on paper. These were the elements of the plan which still had to be built.

The neighbors could not understand all these goings-on with tape and level, sticks and string. They couldn't understand why the newcomers spent their week ends in the dining room, drawing on the table, instead of out in the yard renovating the lawn and trimming the shrubs. The place did look rather neglected during this planning period. The Overbees were much too engrossed in the plan to notice or care.

Finally, on a Saturday morning, they went over the plan for the last time. Then they got out the bank book and made a different kind of survey. They figured long and hard. Then they went back over the plan and broke it down very carefully in terms of the various kinds of materials and skills required to carry it out on the ground. They determined which of these they could supply themselves and which would have to be bought or hired. They debated whether it would be better to install area by area—patio, carport, work yard, etc.—or skill by skill—carpentry, concrete, planting, etc.

They decided on a combination of both. The back yard had to be lowered about one foot at the rear line, and the dirt thus excavated was to be carried around to the front to raise the elevation by a foot. This produced a more usable level platform around the house, and eliminated its slight feeling of sliding down hill. Then all the concrete work—footings for porch and roof extension, and about 2,000 sq. ft. of paving needed to eliminate fussy grass maintenance and provide usable dry clean surfaces—was contracted out in one lump. This broke the bank, leaving the Overbee family with all the carpentry, planting and miscellaneous work to carry out in their spare time.

These new kinds of activity were even more strange than the planning stage. But at least they represented constructive activity which apparently would improve the grounds. The neighbors relaxed into friendly sidewalk superintendence, and there were numerous good-natured debates over whys, wherefores, and hows.

In the meantime the Newfields were beginning to reap the harvest of
hasty landscaping without planning or forethought. With the exception
of one nice lilac by the front door, practically all of their shrubs seemed
to be the wrong plants in the wrong places. Those in front of the windows
threw up clusters of vigorous shoots 6 ft. high, threatening to cut off light
from the rooms and views from within them. The shrubs in front of the
bare walls stubbornly refused either to grow or to die, or put out only a few
tentative horizontal shoots. Some of those on the north side were thin and
yellow, and some on the south side were burned to a crisp. The seeding
of grass over all the level open spaces—front, back, and sides—(which
seemed such a simple way of getting the ground covered) had left the
family saddled with an impossible burden of mowing, watering, and
weeding.

Even the trees seemed to be wrong. The fine lusty maple north of the
patio would provide too much shade where it wasn't needed, while the
lovely flowering plum in the front yard would never shade that sunny
area enough. The 10-ft. flagstone terrace was quite inadequate for the
family's social life, and the 5-ft. wall gave them no real privacy. Mother
and Father Newfield grew more and more annoyed and frustrated. Something had gone wrong with their happy new home. The garden very
definitely was not up to the house.

At this point the Newfields received an invitation, along with most of
the other neighbors, to an open house in the Overbee's new patio. This
structure, especially since it had been enclosed with a rather handsome
wooden screen, had been a subject of considerable curious gossip in the
Newfield household. They had been too engrossed with their own problems to investigate, but they accepted the invitation eagerly. As Father
Newfield said, it was about time for a little socializing with the neighbors.

The new patio was a refreshing experience. The floor of the old porch
had been extended with similar, thicker flooring, and both old and new
painted a rich, dark terra cotta red. The frame of the old porch had likewise been extended with posts and beams, forming an arbor wired to
receive a couple of newly-planted wistaria vines. Holes had been left in
the new floor to preserve a couple of fine old specimen shrubs from the
original planting. The new wooden screen enclosed the patio completely,
6 ft. high, leaving only a gateway from the driveway to the house corner.
This screen was painted olive green, and the posts and beams of arbor
and porch roof a light lemon yellow. What remained of the front yard was
planted in shrubs and ground cover, which would soon isolate the patio
still more from the street. Comfortable fixed benches were hung on the
inside of the wooden screen, in addition to the movable porch furniture.

There was even a large metal bowl on thin legs, filled with bright petunias. To those who remembered the drab front yard of the old house, this was a new adventure in space for living.

The Newfields were torn between admiration and envy. The Overbees had worked no harder than they—although over a longer period—but somehow had more to show for their work. The Newfields studied the full plan, colored with Daughter's crayolas, which was tacked up in the living room. They went home filled with debate, confusion, coffee and cake. This idea of planning was new to them. They had always just gone out and done things when they were ready.

A few nights later they called on the Overbees and spent an evening in energetic conversation. They picked through the clipping collection and borrowed a couple of books. The ideas began to sink in. They looked at their place with new eyes. Mr. Newfield began to toy with possible improvements. He hadn't quite caught up with the over-all plan yet.

At this point two more startling things happened to them. Mrs. Newfield found herself pregnant. This meant that within a year their new house would be too small for them. And Mr. Newfield received notice of a modest legacy from a recently deceased maiden aunt.

Debate now grew even more energetic in the Newfield household. They knew from their previous search that adequate houses were hard to find in Suburbtown. Besides, they liked the neighborhood, and were tired of moving around. The lot next door was just as empty as ever. Henry Overbee had read them several articles about the possibilities of complete planning of modern house and garden together. These were full of magical phrases like "climate control," "space experience," "the nature of materials," and so on. He had spoken in glowing terms of a new young architect in town, who was doing remarkable things with limited budgets. Only the extreme limitations of their own budget had kept the Overbee family from a more complete project. It happened that this particular professional had also studied and learned to respect landscape architecture.

The Newfields decided on a bold adventure. They would sell their house, buy the lot next door, hire the young architect, and build themselves a really up-to-date home. "How crazy can we get?" they asked, looking at each other with admiring eyes. They were impetuous people: once a decision was made things had to move.

It wasn't long before they found themselves under the battered elm in the vacant lot next door, debating with the young architect the pros and cons of saving the tree by building the house around it. They analyzed the lot from front to back, they made a 1-ft. contour survey of its mild undulations, they studied the neighboring houses on all four sides intensely, and they dug holes 4 ft. deep to find out what kind of soil and subsoil they had. They wrote a program several pages long, covering all their wants, needs, desires, and prohibitions, indoors and out.

This story of the production of house plans and of the constructed house by a combination of collaboration and competition between client, architect, and contractor has been written many times in the house and garden press. We need not go into it here in detail. We can now leave the Newfields with their dream house coming true, and the Overbees with their adaptation of dreams to practical reality. No doubt they will continue to help each other as good neighbors should. So much for the fable, now for the moral:

If you analyze your problems, study your techniques and materials, and make and follow a rational plan, the result will be a comfortable and aesthetically satisfying background for your family's indoor and outdoor living activities. Let's take a look at your house, real, imagined, or blue-printed:

How does the front yard look as you cross it?
Is it difficult to get from the sidewalk to the front door?
Is it difficult to get cars in and out of the garage?

The American Home

Max Yavno

Adapted from *Architectural Record*

Outdoors-indoors?

Indoors-outdoors?

Adapted from *Domus*

Where can the guests park?

Is the front yard too large (or too small) in relation to the rest of the lot?

Does the front yard require too much care?

These questions get even more complicated in the back yard, where home owners seldom take full advantage of the possibilities for private use and enjoyment. In this book we want to suggest to you how you might go about achieving some or all of the possibilities of the lot on which your house is or will be built.

What sort of possibilities are we talking about? Here are some of them:

What do we mean by "outdoor living"? Is it really an extension or expansion of indoor living? If so, do you want any? How much can you have if you do want it?

Can you have a beautiful home which is little or no trouble to keep up? Or, if you enjoy gardening, how can you plan your place so that you will have just the amount and kind of gardening you want and no more?

If you are not interested in going outdoors at all, can your garden space still make a contribution to your indoor living, in terms of what you see out through the windows?

Is a garden made just by planting, or is it possible, as cartoons sometimes suggest, to make one out of green concrete?

Can you have a garden full of color all or most of the year without being or hiring an expert gardener? Does this color have to come from flowers?

How can you emphasize and frame good views, screen out bad ones, or create your own rich and spacious picture if there is nothing outside the lot to look at?

How can you make a back yard feel as private and livable as the living room inside the house?

How can you get full beauty—rich, spacious, varied, interesting—into your own home surroundings?

How much is your front yard for you, and how much for the neighborhood?

These and many more questions are involved in your apparently simple decisions as to what to do with the front and back yards. Such problems may have been in your mind when you picked up this book, or we may be suggesting them to you. At any rate, the process of deciding on what kind of landscaping to do begins with finding out what kind of problems this landscaping has to solve. The central problem is to discover how much use and pleasant experience the outdoor space around your home can be made to provide for you.

Frederick Langhorst, architect; photo by Dean Stone

Photo by Julius Shulman; copyright Condé
Nast Publications, Inc.

Morley Baer

If yours is fortunate enough to be one of the thousands of American families planning new homes today, you should be concerned not only with the outdoor space around the house, but with the way the house is planned on the lot. We will find as we investigate further that this has a great deal to do with the possible use and enjoyment of the whole lot.

In order to make this survey of landscaping problems and solutions as complete as possible, we will cover the following ground:

1. The general factors which are basic to all landscape problems across the entire country. These include climate, topography, vegetation (native, agricultural, ornamental), soils; neighborhoods, lot sizes, house sizes, house forms, house plans; family composition, income, and attitudes.

2. The general control of the average or typical home, including both house and garden in one planning unit for maximum efficiency and most complete results.

3. A series of case studies will show the application of such complete home-planning thinking to real problems.

4. The design of the detailed control elements of the home grounds will comprise the main body of the book. First the foundations: grading, drainage, soil conditioning, and utilities. Then the surfacing or floor treatments: paving, lawn, ground covers or cultivation; then the enclosure or side elements of the garden room, both structural and planted; then shelter elements constructed or planted, and finally the detailed enriching or furnishing elements.

5. A special chapter will discuss plants and planting in detail.

6. Another chapter will discuss the procedures for accomplishing all this planning and design: how to go about arranging and organizing the steps from site and program through design, construction, and installation to management.

7. A brief final section will discuss the relationship between home and neighborhood as it affects the life of each family.

Land

Garrett Eckbo

Buildings

Los Angeles Chamber of Commerce

People

Julius Shulman

2. Problems

What are your problems?

Successful gardening? Outdoor living? Pictures from windows? Play space for the children? Where to put clotheslines, garbage cans, incinerators? What to do with the front yard? How to reduce maintenance? How to screen out bad views and provide good ones? Climate control? Beauty with utility? Utility with beauty?

You will find that your landscape planning will go much more smoothly if you begin by sitting down and analyzing your problems:

What problems does the land present?

What problems does the house create on the land?

What problems exist in the neighborhood? Is it getting better, or worse?

What do you need in the yard? What do you *want*, even if you don't need it?

What can you afford? What can you do yourself, if you can't afford to have it done for you?

These questions can go on and on, and accumulate into more and more confusion. We must find ways to fit them into a sensible and orderly picture. Such a picture will establish our planning boundaries, and within them we can relax and give our romantic imaginations full rein.

Landscaping problems are basically of three types. They come from *the land itself*, its natural conditions and materials. They come from *the structures and buildings* that have been or can be put on the land (both yours and your neighbors'). And they come from the *people* who live in the buildings and on the land.

It is extremely unlikely that you have exactly the same combination of landscaping problems as anyone else, but everyone planning the outdoor part of his home is concerned with land, buildings, and people. Your land problems (including climate) will be very similar to your neighbor's, but your family may be more like one on the other side of the Mississippi, and your house like the one your friend built across town. Perhaps an examination of variations of these problems across the country will help you see how you and your house and lot fit into the general picture. The following pages present a sort of cafeteria of landscaping problems. Pick yours out as you go along; you may find some you didn't know you had!

Problems of Land

Since we are discussing problems of *land*scaping, it is not surprising that our first and largest classification should be problems related to land— the actual physical characteristics of your property. These include climate, topography, vegetation, and soils. Let's examine them in turn.

CLIMATE. Everybody likes to talk about the weather. This is sensible, because weather affects our lives more than any other single natural factor. Weather happens every day; the climate is simply the typical annual pattern of different kinds of weather for a particular section of the country. Thus we speak of the East as a *humid* climate, the West as *dry*, the North as *cold*, and the South as *warm*.

Just how do these variations in climate affect our landscaping activities? How does climate affect the way people use their gardens? People who love to putter with plants may regard weather as a challenge, and try to see what can be produced because of or in spite of it. Nongardeners usually want maintenance reduced to a minimum interference with other activities and with the household budget. If they belong to the outdoor type, they also want the climate modified to encourage pleasant surroundings for their favorite outdoor occupations. Even the indoor type has a stake in the weather, because of its effect on views from the windows.

For further data on the nation-wide relations between climate and garden life you might want to examine the 1941 Yearbook of the Department of Agriculture, CLIMATE AND MAN; CLIMATE AND ARCHITECTURE, by Jeffrey Aronin; or CLIMATIC ATLAS OF THE UNITED STATES, by Visher.

Temperature affects both plants and people: both need special treatment if it goes above or below the range in which they are most comfortable. The range of minimum winter temperatures—average and lowest ever—establishes the northern boundary for each kind of plant—and many people. As the temperature range reaches upper and lower extremes, our choice of kinds of plants becomes smaller (this may be a blessing) and the problems of protecting our own bodies become greater. The transition from the region of cold and stormy winters to the milder region where broad-leaved evergreens will grow in quantity is marked across the country by a belt of average minimum temperatures ranging from 5 to 10 degrees above zero.

Precipitation affects plants even more directly than it does people. Most garden plants will fail unless there is enough rainfall, evenly distributed throughout the growing season. Artificial watering is often needed to supplement natural precipitation, particularly for green ground cover, flower borders, and choice specimen shrubs and trees.

The amount of precipitation varies widely from one part of the United States to another. The eastern half of the country is humid, averaging over 25 in. of rainfall annually, while the western half, except for a few spots in the mountains, is almost entirely semiarid to arid, with less than 25 in. per year. Through the center of the country, from Minnesota and North Dakota south to Texas, runs a dividing strip where the climate over the years ranges from humid to semiarid.

Although the highest precipitation in the country is registered in the Pacific Northwest, the bulk of this rainfall is recorded during the winter, when it is too cold for most plants to grow; hence the whole Pacific Coast is said to have a "summer-dry" climate. In the entire western half of the country, the only way to avoid artificial watering is to use native material, or other plants which will adjust themselves to local conditions. Even so, it would usually be necessary to eliminate green cover and flowers, at least during the dry season.

The dry-country landscape is very different from the humid-country landscape, unless a more or less synthetic climate can be produced within a limited area. Within dry country we also have differing *cold-dry* and *warm-dry* landscapes, and within humid country we have *cold-humid* and *warm-humid* landscapes. These four are our basic landscape regions. Have you plotted the one where your property belongs?

Humidity, the measure of moisture in the atmosphere, is also a measure of livability for both plants and animals, and is related to precipitation. (When humidity reaches 100 per cent, it rains.) However, humidity must be considered in relation to temperature. Although July humidity is just about the same in San Francisco as in New York, we can stand the San Francisco humidity more easily because there the July temperatures are 10 to 15 degrees lower.

Natural landscape regions of the United States

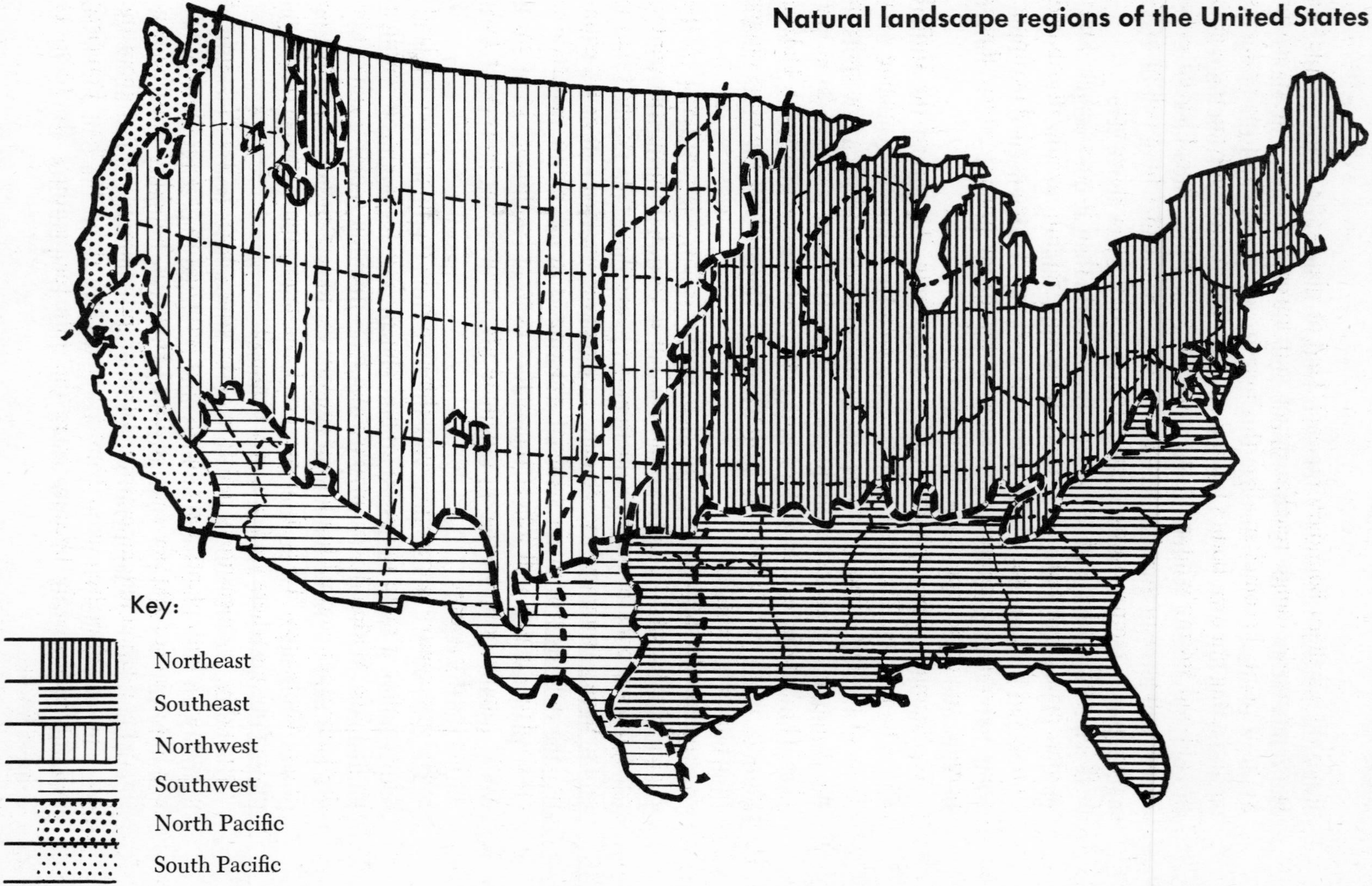

Key:
- Northeast
- Southeast
- Northwest
- Southwest
- North Pacific
- South Pacific

Sunshine, of course, is as essential as precipitation to growing things. Beautiful landscapes can be produced with either maximum or minimum light, but they are quite different kinds of landscapes. The amount of light affects not only plants, but also people: our general personal comfort and the way we look at the landscape. Hence a psychological element is introduced into our planning. Heavy fog and desert glare are extremes which lead us to appreciate more temperate and moderate light conditions. Thus, in regions of heavy dull weather we try to design landscapes which lighten and liven the atmosphere, and in dry, glaring climates we use many trees and structural shade elements to temper and diffuse the light.

Frost determines the quality and quantity of vegetation in a region, provided moisture and other conditions are adequate, because frost-free periods are the growing season for plants. These periods are also rough measures of the percentage of the year in which outdoor living without special protection is possible. However, since warm weather may encourage insects and unpleasant winds as well as plants, we can see that other more complicated control problems may be involved in plans for outdoor living.

CLIMATIC REGIONS.   Thus we find that our country can be divided into certain rather definite regions in terms of the kind of landscape development which the general climate seems to call for:

1. *The humid Northeast,* with definite summer and winter seasons and their attendant garden problems, about which more has been written than any other part of the country.
2. *The humid Southeast,* the Old South of song and story, the home of the gardenia, magnolia, and sub-tropical palms.
3. *The semiarid to arid Northwest:* prairie, great plain, mountain, and desert; most variable and unpredictable as to weather, generally dependent upon artificial irrigation for successful horticulture if not agriculture; least developed or analyzed in terms of landscape development.
4. *The arid to semiarid Southwest,* running from Texas west to the California deserts.
5. *The summer-dry Pacific Coast,* a broadleaf evergreen zone from north to south, which nevertheless divides itself approximately at Eureka, Calif., with the Northwest both wetter and colder in winter than the Southwest. This difference is sufficient to produce notable variations in typical plant material between the two portions.
6. *The moderately tropical Hawaiian Islands.*
7. *The generally severe climate of Alaska* (more temperate in the southeast sector).

Local variations, of course, occur within these primary regions. These correspond to differences in latitude within the region, in altitude (as we go up we go north in climate), and in proximity to large bodies of water, which modify the climate considerably. (See THE WORLD BOOK on U.S. climate, Sunset's WESTERN GARDEN GUIDE, "Microclimatology," *Architectural Forum*, March, 1947, and various articles by Dudley in recent issues of *House Beautiful*.)

We have continuously smaller and more specific units of variation, until we get down to microclimate, which includes the actual variations in climate in every community and on every site. Everyone who has ever worked with planting has experienced these changes and complexities between high and low, slope and flat, pocket and alley, north side and south side, east side and west side, near water and away from it. Cold spots, drafts, the north slope, the hollow where cold air collects, the west slope or wall, the exposed ridge—all of these, combined with local variations in depth and quality of soil, can baffle the designer with the fine regular plan, and lend support to the cause for wild gardens and naturalism. As Fitch says:

> For the rude and pressing needs of the individual deal with his immediate environment—conditions within his apartment block, or place of work. Detailed knowledge at this scale is almost totally lacking in this country. . . . It is the character and juxtaposition of air masses which determine the weather in a given locality at a given time. But the local behavior of these air masses is in turn affected by the particular configuration of the land: the height and depth of its hills and valleys; the shapes, sizes, and densities of the buildings upon it; its bodies of water, groves of trees, parks, and paved streets; finally, by the way the sun falls upon the whole ensemble.
>
> It thus follows that every change we make upon the landscape—every house we raise or tree we cut down, each field we plow or street we pave—affects the microclimate. This change may be small; it will certainly be definite. . . .

TOPOGRAPHY.   Landscape problems vary with the slope of the ground. In order to feel secure and well balanced, we have to hold ourselves vertical, in line with the center of the earth and the pull of gravity. When we speak of the slope of the ground we refer to the angle the ground surface makes with this vertical line. Dead level ground, which almost never occurs in nature, is at right angles, or 90 degrees, to this vertical. As this angle decreases we have greater difficulty in maintaining our balance upon it, and this is why surfaces which are most nearly level are most useful and comfortable for us.

Local variations in climate

from PLANNING THE GARDEN by Robert B. Deering, University of California at Davis

Consider direction of wind.

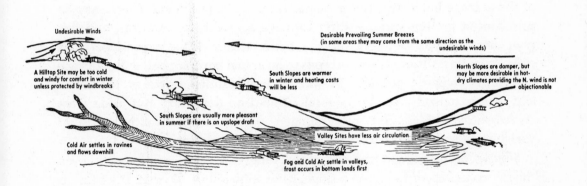

Best location for an inland home site is generally part way up a slope that faces the desirable direction. This will depend upon prevailing wind, sun, and the views.

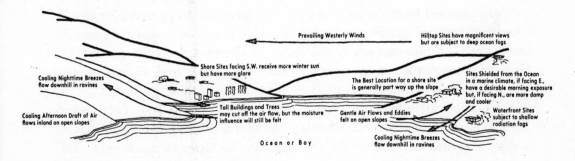

The combination of topography and exposure may determine the desirability of a coastal site. Generally, best location for a shore site is part way up a slope.

Since water, as well as people, responds to gravity, its movements and all of its beneficial or harmful effects on the land are conditioned by slope. The ground itself moves or is stable in response to the force of gravity, assisted by moving water. Even plants grow and balance themselves against the downward pull, and structures made by man are considered well-built if the floors are dead level and the walls plumb vertical.

Slopes. Slopes, in landscape practice, can be divided roughly into three groups in terms of the problems they create: Flat, sloping, and steep.

Flat ground (or ground which seems flat) has less than 5 ft. of vertical fall in each 100 ft. measured horizontally. Even this much slope, however, may be obvious against a truly horizontal wall or building. This "flat" ground is of course the easiest to develop for outdoor use, especially within the limits of the average home site, but even flat land has its problems. There may be problems of getting surface water to move across it, for example, and this poor drainage may be aggravated by the tendency of the more impervious soils—from fine, silty soils and subsoils to an actual hardpan below the surface —to collect on flatter ground. (By way of compensation, however, the better and deeper topsoils are also generally found on flat land.) But aside from considerations of comfort and drainage, the mere need for interest and variety may prompt us to change slopes or levels by design.

Sloping or rolling ground, on which one can move comfortably even though conscious of being on a slope, runs up to about 10 or 12 ft. of fall in 100 horizontal. This kind of topography is generally most interesting and fruitful to develop, and it offers great possibilities for combining practicality and imagination in the handling of ground and structural forms. Drainage is easily handled, although moving water must be controlled to avoid erosion. Extra construction or grading is needed to make these slopes useful and pleasant, and entails extra labor—hired or your own—but if the solutions are properly planned from the beginning, extra dividends in pleasure can result. (See discussion of grading, Chapter 5.) This does not mean that equally interesting and pleasant solutions cannot be developed on flat ground, but such solutions require more architectural imagination, and do not grow as naturally out of existing conditions as do plans for sloping ground.

Steep slopes include all those above 12 per cent (12 ft. in 100). On these we have so much difficulty in maintaining our balance or moving about that we are more or less uncomfortable. Development of steep slopes is quite diffi- cult, and costs more than either flat or sloping ground. Houses can be built on slopes up to 30 per cent, but a great deal of engineering ingenuity is needed to build them successfully. Soils are apt to be thin or bad on steep slopes, especially as they get higher above valley floors, and rocky conditions are more common. However, once these extra difficulties and costs are

1

Steep

Sloping

2

Flat

3

Vertical

100% 1:1 — 45° (cut slopes)

50% 2:1 — 27° (fill slopes)

30% 3:1 — 18°   **1**
(maximum for construction)

10% 10:1 — 5¾° (steep)   **2**
5% 20:1 — 3° (rolling)
0% (dead level)   **3**

Force of gravity to center of the earth

accepted, steep sites can produce the most dramatic and exciting internal arrangement and outside views. These sites are likely to require structural or architectural solutions, and are difficult to develop usefully by grading or planting alone.

All three types of slope, at the scale of residential lots, can be found in almost every part of the country, sometimes even on the same lot. Although the West is generally rough and mountainous it has many large valleys and plains, and the Midwest, which is commonly considered flat, has rolling sections and breaks for streams and river beds. The East, as we know, is full of variable topography, though seldom as rough as the West.

Prevalence of soil or rock also affects landscape development problems. Rock forms are usually rough and angular; soil forms smooth and curved. Although both are to be found throughout the country, the soft curved forms are somewhat more typical of humid regions, and rough angular forms of arid or mountainous regions. Soil, of course, is easier to move or change than rock, and natural rock outcrops or ledges are apt to remain in place and have gardens or houses built around them. Remember, though, that there are no lovelier forms in nature than the flowing curved planes of maturely weathered rolling hills. These forms are equally inspiring, and equally in need of preservation and repair. Unfortunately they are also the chief casualty of most hillside housing developments.

VEGETATION. Landscaping processes tend to concentrate, at times too much and too soon, on planting. But late or soon, the planting we do is conditioned to a great extent by the vegetation in the region around us. This can be classified into three primary types: *native, agricultural,* and *ornamental.*

Native vegetation existed before we came, and still exists, either in spite of us or with our help. It varies with climate and topography, and each major climatic region has a "plant formation" consisting of the plants best adapted to flourish there. (See CLIMATE AND VEGETATION, by Blumenstock and Thornwaite, on page 105 of CLIMATE AND MAN, for a fuller discussion of these relationships.)

Agricultural vegetation is introduced and developed to provide certain crops which we need. Like natural vegetation, it is also related to soil and climate. Field crops, fruit crops, livestock, poultry farming, and mixed farming all produce their typical rural landscapes, and each affects the landscaping problems on the grounds of neighboring homes.

Ornamental vegetation is developed to solve certain functional problems, such as ground cover or windbreak, but even more for the visual pleasure it affords. It is broader and more flexible in content than the other two types, and can draw from both of them.

Garrett Eckbo

Union Pacific Railroad photo

Earth forms | Rock forms

Native   Agricultural   Ornamental

Union Pacific Railroad photo   Sunkist photo   Shulman; courtesy Condé Nast

Grasses, flowering plants, and other herbaceous ground covers, shrubs, desert plants, vines, and trees of various forms and sizes are all utilized for ornamental purposes, and regardless which of these dominates the local wild or rural landscape we tend to want most or all of them in our gardens. They complete the balanced and harmonious landscape which we need for comfort and peace of mind.

Most of the activities of horticulture are concerned with determining the maximum variety of plants that can be grown in a given climatic region, and improving each suitable type of plant so that it will do its best within the region. Thus ornamental vegetation may include anything from native plants which will grow with no care at all to delicate exotics which require the most skillful care in order to survive. Obviously the plants requiring the least care for the most show will be the most commonly planted, and the amount of time and skill the gardener commands should be a factor in the selection of his material.

When care is available, however, it is interesting to work creatively, introducing into the landscape new material which improves it and renders it more humanly livable. Such a purpose is just as fine as that of expressing the native landscape in a more poetic way. In the Southwest, where native vegetation tends toward dull grays and browns, the strong dark or clear greens of plants from more humid areas (grown with irrigation) are a welcome relief and contrast, and definitely render the climate more livable. In grasslands and prairies we plant trees; in forests we clear open spaces and plant grass; in the desert we introduce both trees and grass. All of these changes have the function of equalizing, improving, and humanizing these landscapes, making them better places for us to live.

SOILS. The classification of soils relates directly to climate, for the two principal classes are soils of humid climates, or *pedalfers,* and soils of arid climates, or *pedocals.* As would be expected, pedalfers prevail in the eastern half of the United States, and pedocals in the West. Where moisture is present, the soil remains moist down to the permanent water table, and forests are the natural vegetation. Gradually or rapidly, however, nutrients in the soil are washed away, and must often be replenished. Dry soils, on the other hand, in which grasses, brush, and shrubs grow naturally, are rich in nutrients but poor in water. Actually more money is spent on irrigation in the West than on fertilizers in the East.

Within the two great classes there are many groups of soils and local variations. A more complete discussion of soil types will be found in GEO-MORPHOLOGY, by Lobeck, and "Climate and Soil," by Charles Kellogg, page 265 of CLIMATE AND MAN.

Soil map of the United States

from CLIMATE AND MAN, 1941 Yearbook of Agriculture

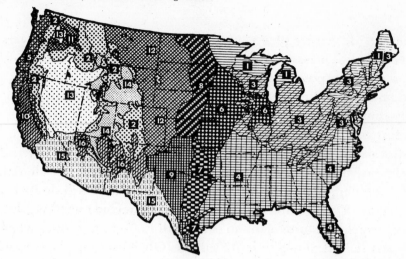

Note how the pattern parallels our regional map.

Soil conditioning

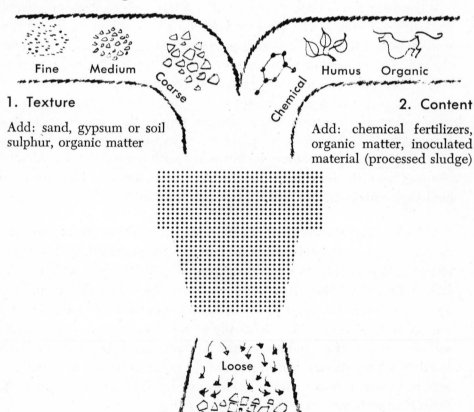

Fine   Medium   Coarse

1. Texture

Add: sand, gypsum or soil sulphur, organic matter

Chemical   Humus   Organic

2. Content

Add: chemical fertilizers, organic matter, inoculated material (processed sludge)

Loose

Tight

3. Drainage

Add: sand and/or rock, mechanical drains (horizontal or vertical), organic matter, deep cultivation

For planting we are concerned with three properties of soil: *texture, content,* and *drainage.*

1. *Texture* ranges from sand (coarse) to clay (fine). A medium, loamy texture is generally best, and we try to modify these extremes toward this ideal by soil conditioning.

2. *Content* concerns the quantities and proportions of chemical nutrients, but even more the amounts of humus (rotted vegetation) and soil bacteria. A proper balance between chemical and organic is important. Western soils tend to be high in chemical and low in organic, and Eastern the reverse.

3. *Drainage* refers to how rapidly water moves vertically through the soil. This depends on texture and looseness, both near the surface and some distance below it. Friable loam has the best drainage, neither too fast nor too slow. Water should stay around the roots of most plants long enough to give them a good drink, but not long enough to drown them. There are, of course, kinds of plants which will do well in fast or slow drainage or other bad soil conditions, but it is generally best to improve the soil if possible.

With soils we complete the survey of the complex problems which originate with the land. These are the gardener's problems, which are solved by that combination of know-how, intuition, and sympathy generally known as the Green Thumb.

Problems of Structural Development

Now we turn to the problems produced by building and structural development. Although these differ less in different parts of the country than the natural problems, they are generally more difficult to solve, and the solutions are seldom completely successful.

NEIGHBORHOODS. Your home may be in the city, with small lots, large buildings, houses connected in rows, perhaps more than one family per lot, heavy traffic, and a confusion of commercial and industrial activities around it. Or you may live in the suburbs or a small uncrowded town, with lots 50 ft. wide or more, mostly detached, single-family houses, light traffic, and a separation from commercial and industrial districts; or on a farm or in the woods, mountains or desert, with your nearest neighbor so far away as to be hard to reach when you want him.

Max Yavno

Urban

M. Halberstadt

Suburban

Union Pacific Railroad photo (2)

Rural

Primeval

Each of these neighborhoods has its own living problems, and therefore its own landscape problems. These varying problems come from such questions as these:

1. How many neighbors do you have, and how close together do they live? Are they breathing down your neck, or do you rarely see them?
2. What community facilities, such as shopping, services, recreation, education, and religion are conveniently available? Do you have to make up on your own property for those that are missing?
3. What kind of housing surrounds your home? Apartments? Row houses? Detached houses?
4. Are there other types of land use and buildings, such as manufacturing, commercial, recreational, institutional, or agricultural in your immediate neighborhood? How do they affect your living conditions?

In short, what kind of neighborhood surrounds your lot? How much of it do you want to see?

LOTS. Every lot, of course, may have a different solution for the neighborhood problems surrounding it, even though the same problems may affect an entire subdivision. Let's take a look at the individual problems involved in the lots themselves.

Lot sizes vary a great deal, but they fall roughly into five groups:

small	25 x 100 ft. and less	1/16 acre or less
medium	50 x 100 ft.	1/8 acre
large	100 x 100 ft.	1/4 acre
extra large	100 x 200 ft.	1/2 acre
estate or farm	200 x 200 ft.	1 or more acres

Lots within each of these groups tend to have similar problems, at least if the size of house and slope of ground are similar.

The shapes of lots are quite variable, and produce some of the most specialized landscape problems. The shapes result from a subdivision process which visually has little connection with the design of the houses that will occupy the lots, and even less with the garden design. At best, the subdivider assumes that his lots will be adequate for the type of houses he assumes will be built. What he has in mind is usually the dullest, most unimaginative, and least flexible kind of standardized house design.

Logically, of course, house, garden, and subdivision design should proceed at the same time. One might then hope that the lot spaces around each house would be adequate for its outdoor needs.

The shape of the lot is most important on flat or gently sloping land; on steeper sites the topography will assume a larger importance. Most lots are

Small

Large

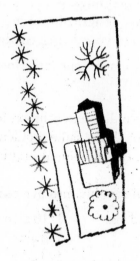

Long-narrow

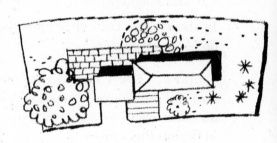

Short-wide

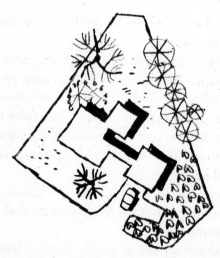

Pie-shaped: Street at wide end

Pie-shaped: Street at narrow end

Lots are quite variable.

rectangular, but the proportions between width and depth will vary. In
general, shallow lots present more difficult design problems than deep lots,
especially if the back yard is wider than its depth. No minimum dimensions
can be given, because these depend on the size and shape of the house. Each
house requires a lot of certain dimensions to make possible its best outdoor
extension. The moral practice of designing the house to fit the lot is really
putting the cart before the horse. Irregular lots can also be judged in terms
of over-all width and depth, with attention to where maximum and minimum dimensions fall. A pie-shaped lot which is narrow at the street and
wide at the rear is generally more desirable than the reverse.

Orientation of lots in relation to sun, wind, cold-air drainage, and views is
quite variable. In the northern half of the country the possibility of opening
the main glass walls of the house to the south will simplify problems of climate control. In the southern half a northern orientation may be better. East
or west exposures are apt to require special protection from low sun. Prevailing winds and breezes during cold and warm seasons have great influence on livability. Elevated lots are more exposed to wind and sun. Low
spots collect cold air. A choice between panoramic or more restricted views
must be related to these other factors.

HOUSES. The sizes of houses vary almost as much as those of lots. Although they are usually classified by number of rooms or square footage, it
is also well to consider the proportion of the total lot area they cover. One-
story houses cover more land than two-story houses with a like number of
rooms, but they also put all of the rooms close to the garden. Different kinds
of landscape problems go with houses of one, two, and three or more bedrooms because of the different types of families that live in them. In terms
of area, houses can be classified as follows:

Small:	Under 1,000 sq. ft.
Medium:	1,000 to 2,000 sq. ft.
Large:	2,000 to 3,000 sq. ft.
Extra large:	Over 3,000 sq. ft.

House forms or shapes also vary a great deal, from simple boxes with only
four corners to irregular ramblers with innumerable corners, angles, and
curves. In these days of experimental building, the proportion of solid walls
to windows to doors is quite variable. Roof pitches or slopes vary from steep
to flat, and also vary in forms from simple gables to complicated hips. Over-
hangs vary from nothing to many feet.

Houses can be classified or grouped according to these simple characteristics much better than by vague abstractions such as "style," and houses of

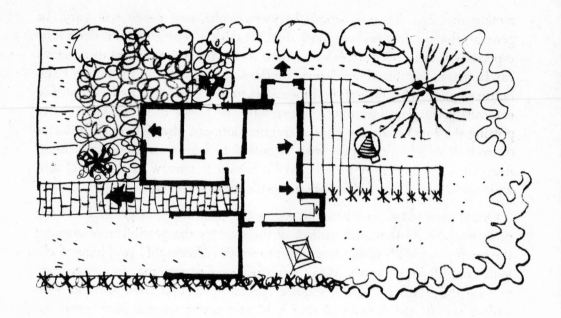

Closed

Plan

Open

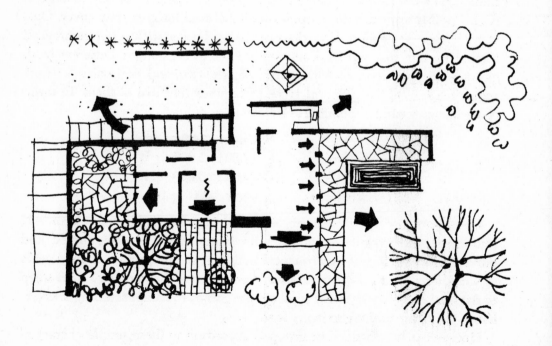

different forms of wall and roof and number of openings do produce different landscape problems. They do this because the outside of the house makes one or more sides of the garden room we are developing. Actually the form of the house should evolve from the natural conditions. We should have house forms suited to our various climatic regions, rather than equal parts of Cape Cod cottages, ranch houses, and California bungalows distributed from coast to coast.

House plans are quite variable. From our landscape point of view we are mainly concerned with how they are connected or related to the outdoor portions of the lots around them:

1. Is it easy to get in and out of the house, and to see out of the windows?
2. How many rooms have outside doors?
3. Are all portions of the lot easy to reach and use?
4. Do the larger portions of the yard connect directly with the larger (living) portions of the house?
5. What do the main windows look at?
6. What do the main doors lead to or from?
7. How far is the floor level of the house from the ground level outside?

These variables affect architectural design as well as landscape design, and they affect the design of new houses as well as the remodeling of old ones. These questions are not intended to imply that more doors and windows are necessarily better than fewer, or that floors close to the ground are better than floors high above it. They only produce different kinds of relations between houses and gardens.

House materials vary a good deal. This variation increases with the ways in which they are combined and treated. The basic materials are these:

1. Masonry (stone, brick, concrete)
2. Wood (painted or natural)
3. Stucco (smooth or textured, neutral or colored)
4. Glass

These materials affect landscape design in terms of continuity (extending the house materials into the garden to tie them together) or in terms of contrast (using different materials in the garden to set the house off and frame it). These are important landscape decisions.

We begin to see now why landscape problems, which are so simple when explained on a blackboard, are so complicated in the field. Each of these groups of variables we have mentioned is fairly simple in itself. But when they are all combined, the possibilities are endless! And almost every combination does seem to occur somewhere at some time.

Problems of People

Finally we come to the varying problems produced by the people in the buildings on the land. Basically we are all in search of approximately the same things in our home environments. These are thought of as part of the American standard of living. They include, in the most general terms:

1. A house adequate in size, construction, and equipment for family needs
2. A large lot, flat enough for the development of pleasant garden surroundings
3. A nice surrounding neighborhood.

Throughout the country, the way the property is developed to meet these standards varies quite consistently with the financial resources of individual families.

Variation with climate is not nearly so consistent, for we are only beginning to learn how to apply modern technology and design inspiration to the problems of living in our various climatic regions. Actually, house styles vary more with the owners' tastes than with climate. Spanish, Tudor, and American Colonial houses may appear in the same block in any part of the country. Thus we, the American people, with all our needs and desires, likes and dislikes, are the unifying factor for all the variations in land and climate and structure within our borders, and therefore variations among us are basic to landscape problems.

Composition by age and sex is the first area in which our families vary. We include single persons, couples without children, couples with varying numbers of children, single parents with children, and various relatives combined with any of these. All have different kinds of landscape problems.

The principal difference comes with children. Houses and gardens are completely different with or without them. Frederick Gutheim, in HOUSES FOR FAMILY LIVING, has developed a principle that family problems and needs tend to change in six- to seven-year cycles, as children grow. Preschool, school, adolescent, and college or working-age children introduce their families to different types of living and land use problems. Therefore our designs must not only solve today's problems, but must be flexible enough to adjust themselves to those of tomorrow and the next day as well.

Income level is another area of family variation. The pattern of income distribution may be found in census figures as recorded in THE STATISTICAL ABSTRACT OF THE UNITED STATES, published annually by the United States Government Printing Office. The question as to what is the minimum income for securing a desirable home unit, even with "do-it-yourself" activity,

Colonial

Georgian

Spanish

Los Angeles Chamber of Commerce

"Style"

Ranch

Victorian

Photos by Julius Shulman unless otherwise noted

Modern

must be left to the reader's experience. Although there are many humble homes whose charm and quality exceed that of some costly mansions, by and large we get the kind of design and installation we can afford, unless we are able to do it *well* ourselves. Of course there are those who can afford to buy quality design and workmanship who do not do so for one reason or another, but this is their special problem.

Race, religion, and national origin mark other family variations. Figures on these groups may also be found in THE STATISTICAL ABSTRACT OF THE UNITED STATES. Americans of Negro and Oriental background, plus another four million of Mexican ancestry, represent a rich cultural reservoir. The great Mediterranean—Latin American pattern of patio living comes to us through Mexico. It has had a profound effect upon our thinking as to the relations between house and garden. Chinese and Japanese gardens at their best represent a peak of refined garden design and sensitive use of materials which we have yet to reach. Negro culture in Africa is rich, varied, and integrated with daily life to an extent few of us understand. The American Negro, who now thinks of himself as both American and Negro, has made rich contributions to our American culture in many ways.

Attitudes toward home planning problems also vary from one family to another, and have a tremendous influence upon the landscapes we produce around our homes. For example:

What is your attitude toward gardening? Are you interested, or willing to take part in it? Do you enjoy it? Your answers have a lot to do with the kind of plant growth you will have in your garden.

What is your attitude toward outdoor living? Do you think it possible around your home, in your part of the country? Do you want more, or less of it? This attitude determines which of the possibilities suggested in this book you are able and willing to explore.

What is your attitude toward the quality of things? Do you care whether they are pleasant or beautiful? Whether they make you feel comfortable? Whether they seem to fit together and serve their purpose well? Whether you would miss them if they were removed?

All such attitudes determine how seriously you may take this exploration of landscape possibilities. If you take it seriously enough, you will find there is no end to improvement and to the discovery of new refinements, pleasures, and experiences in landscape arrangements. If your interest is superficial, you may be satisfied with the first quick idea or easy solution that comes to mind, and do very little to improve the environment in which you have been living.

Halberstadt

Julius Shulman

Morley Baer

Royston

Ernest Braun

3. Home Planning

There are few spots in the world where people can live out of doors the year around. Therefore home planning and building involve production of an indoor climate as nearly perfect as possible, in spite of the vagaries of the local weather. Contemporary research and practice show us that garden elements are very important in developing this control of indoor climate. They take some of the load off the structure itself, and create a zone of partially controlled climate in the garden spaces around the house. These then become more livable and useful than the local climate normally allows.

Thus, in addition to providing beautiful settings for the house, and lovely pictures to view out of the windows, garden spaces influence indoor comfort, and during the milder portions of the year can be developed into outdoor extensions of the living spaces of the house.

Home planning then, must include both indoors and outdoors. It is, in fact, a project for complete control of the space we live in, the things we see, and the use and maintenance of that space and those things. This control is only a means to the end of developing the best possible surroundings for family life and individual work and relaxation. All of us, when returning home from work or other expedition, want to feel as we cross the front yard that maximum comfort, happiness, security, and stability await us there. Whether or not it is true that our home is a castle to which we can retire to recover from a difficult and disorderly world, that is the hope in all our minds.

The general problems of such home planning are similar throughout the country. They are similar because human needs and desires are basically similar; it is the surrounding conditions which vary. All homes must provide,

1   Julius Shulman   Roger Sturtevant   2

3   Ernest Braun   Ernest Braun   4

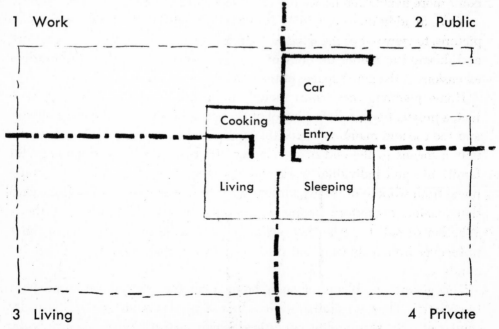

1   Work   2   Public

Car

Cooking   Entry

Living   Sleeping

3   Living   4   Private

Main parts of the home

in one way or another, for four main functions: public access, general living, work space, private living.

Public access includes front yard, walk, driveway, porch or stoop, and entry hall.

General living includes living, dining, library, music, play, rumpus, and family rooms; and patio, terrace, outdoor living room, larger gardens, pools, courts, etc.

Work space includes kitchen, laundry, shop or sewing room, drying and service yard, utility garden, kids' play area, garage, storage, etc.

Private living includes bedroom, bath, dressing, sleeping-porch, suntrap, etc.

Each of these elements works best, and provides most livability and pleasure, when it is planned and built as a continuous indoor-outdoor unit. This idea is contrary to the normal practice of first building the house and then deciding what to do around it. It is also a direct result of all the experience accumulated from that normal practice.

This complete thinking, which includes all of the parts of the home (house plus garden) in one process, helps to eliminate many common planning mistakes which can never be corrected once the buildings are up. Interior and landscape designers spend tremendous amounts of time and energy working out more or less clever solutions for problems which would never have existed if the buildings had been planned and placed properly in relation to the lot space around them, or if the size and form of the lot had been adequate for the particular building.

The need for complete planning is not, however, confined to builders of new homes. As we shall see later (see below, "After the House Is Built"), replanning an existing house also requires a plan embracing indoor and outdoor spaces.

Some of the desirable results which can be guaranteed only by thinking about the development of the whole lot (house and garden) at once, are:

Complete climate control will be achieved. This means control of temperature, precipitation (rain and snow), humidity, wind, light, and insects (a special feature of some climates). Although the house is the primary shelter from the elements, its effectiveness can be greatly increased, as well as its living space expanded, by proper integration with garden elements. Where temperature and light are too high or intense (especially in fall or spring) a zone of filtering elements—trees or lath structures—around the house is often essential. Where temperatures drop too low for comfort, proper combinations of walls and paving can expedite solar heating, and increase the patio season by a month or more at either end. Trees and shrubs disperse

and absorb the impact of rain and snow, and extensions of solid roofing often make possible outdoor living in rainy weather, and also protect the furniture. Wind is best controlled by trees and shrubs or pierced structures,
which absorb it. Solid obstacles merely divert it. Insects, of course, are a
regional or social problem. Outdoors on individual properties they can be
controlled only with screening. The proper use of yellow light outdoors at
night will avoid attracting some, and smoke is an effective repellent.

The front yard will be large enough to separate house and street comfortably, and to make a proper contribution to the appearance of the neighborhood. But it will not be so large as to create an installation or maintenance burden for the owner, or steal needed space from the private livable
portions of the lot. The walk connection between front door and street will
be convenient and hospitable, yet not overdone. The drive connection from
garage to street will be designed in recognition of the way in which auto-
mobiles are driven: how steep a slope they can climb, how much space
they need to turn around in, how tight a turn they can make going forward
or backward, whether it is safe to back into the street, how quickly they
can make the change from a steep climb to a flat shelf, and whether extra
guest parking is needed.

The general living rooms will be so placed as to open upon the main or
largest portion of the lot, as well as the best view and sun or shade. This
will make it possible to connect them directly with whatever terrace, patio,
or outdoor living development you may desire, or to have them overlook
the main garden picture if outdoor living is not important. This will avoid
the classical and continuous mistake of American house planning, which is
to place the living rooms at the front of the house facing the street, and
separated from the rear yard by kitchen, laundry and service porch. More
potential living space has probably been lost through this mistake than
through any other. Quite often, of course, this lost space can be regained
by careful garden design and some remodeling of the house.

The work rooms of the house will be so placed as to connect with yard
space sufficient for clothes-drying, trash and garbage disposal, outdoor work
hobbies, and similar service or somewhat messy activities. Logical elements
to connect with these outdoor work areas are fruit, vegetable, or cut-flower
gardens (which are not necessarily always presentable), children's play areas
(same reason, plus supervision from kitchen and laundry), garage (which
may function as wet weather play space), storage of tools, toys, and other
gear, garden work centers (including potting benches, lath and glass shelters, fertilizer, soil, and compost storage, and so on). These work areas have

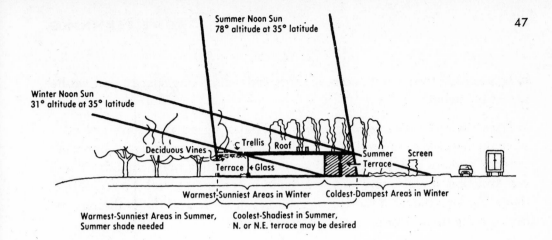

Summer Noon Sun
78° altitude at 35° latitude

Winter Noon Sun
31° altitude at 35° latitude

Deciduous Vines — Trellis — Roof — Summer Terrace — Screen

Terrace — Glass

Warmest-Sunniest Areas in Winter — Coldest-Dampest Areas in Winter

Warmest-Sunniest Areas in Summer,
Summer shade needed

Coolest-Shadiest in Summer,
N. or N.E. terrace may be desired

The angle and sweep of the sun

from PLANNING THE GARDEN by Robert B. Deering, University of California at Davis

Proper orientation dictates how the house and garden should be planned to achieve warm, livable areas in winter and cool ones in summer.

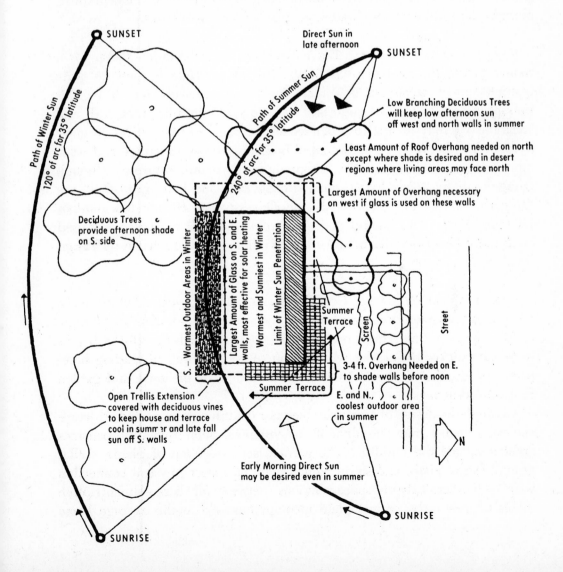

to be screened from front and rear yards and main living spaces, and yet be accessible to both.

Private sleeping and bathing rooms will be so placed as to have at least a pleasant outlook over garden or view. At most they may have connected outdoor porches or enclosed gardens into which they open directly. These can function for sleeping out, sun-bathing, or private relaxation out-of-doors. Perhaps the most radical suggestion is a garden off the bathroom, for drying off in the sun, or even an outdoor shower.

We know very well that these factors of relation between house and lot are not the only, or even necessarily the most important, considerations in house planning. Many other factors, of orientation and structure and plumbing and internal circulation, are primary. But we know from experience that if these factors of lot or outdoor connection are considered at the beginning, along with the others, better and more livable homes will result.

DAILY CIRCULATION. Let us examine the circulation factor for a moment. Life for most of us is busy. Most of our time is spent in quite restricted areas and circulation routes. The things we see and feel during this bulk of our time are most important to us, even though on week ends and vacations we may escape to other scenes, at home or away. The ordinary paths of life—bedroom to bathroom to breakfast corner to garage and work (or school or kitchen, laundry, shopping, and so on), returning through garage to dining room, living room, kitchen, bath and bed again—these are the paths which will benefit most from close study of their indoor-outdoor relations. Each of us should make a careful diagram of these most-used areas and circulation lines in his or her own home, and of what is seen from them inside and out.

THREE DIMENSIONS. Complete home planning, with all of its facets, factors, and considerations, must be approached as three-dimensional design, or space organization. This is probably the point at which the subject begins to be difficult for the reader who has no special training in reading blueprints, or visualizing physical results at the full scale of house and garden from scale drawings.

Although the design of a house, which is a continuous connected structure enclosing rooms, may be difficult to visualize, such difficulty becomes greater outside the building. The garden is a collection of plants, walks, ground forms, pools, and so on, which have no direct physical connection with each other. Talk of "space relations" between all these elements often seems esoteric, arty, or just plain incomprehensible to the average home

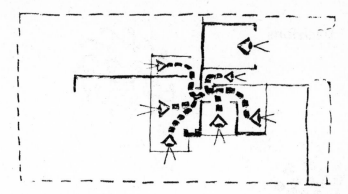

Your daily routes and viewpoints

Your block of air

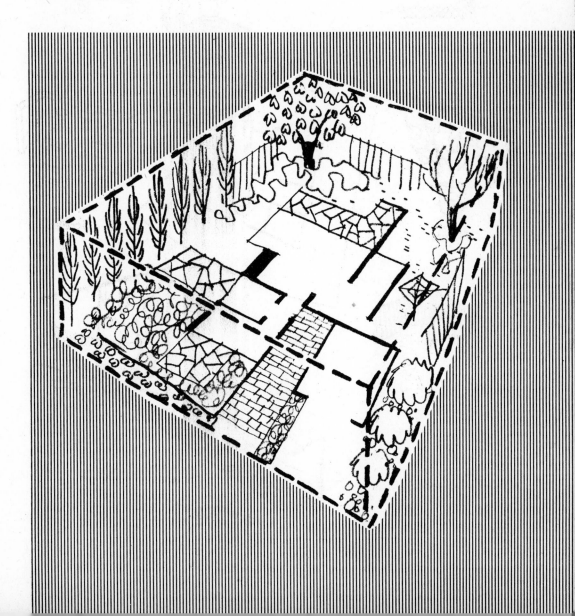

Decisions

Sun

Shade

Kids

Plants

Screen

Dog

Wind

Picture

owner. Yet the functional complete planning which we have discussed cannot be done successfully unless these elements are all thought of as solid objects with height, width, and thickness, and also unless the open space or distance between them is considered as important as the objects themselves.

Each lot, as a piece of real estate, is the bottom, side, or floor of a block of air space in which people may be able to live. The sides of this block are invisible planes which are the vertical projection of the property lines. The top, while not so tangible, is the height to which local zoning ordinances will allow a structure to be built, or the height to which trees may grow.

People live in air as fish live in water. Everything in their lives is conditioned by the quality of this air. The block of air space above our lot or home site has no meaning or livability until it is enclosed and defined with structures and plants. If this is done well, a series of homey rooms will result, and we will settle down to stay. If it is not done well we will never feel right in the place, and sooner or later will move.

Every physical change that occurs on this lot changes the way it feels to us. If we dig a hole, and build a mound with the excavated dirt, it will feel quite different. A carpet of grass, of bricks or of cabbages will each have different results in our feelings. A 3-ft. fence around the boundary will give some sense of enclosure, but not nearly so much as a 10-ft. fence. A continuous grove of trees, a glass roof, or a solid tar-and-gravel roof will each give a different quality of shelter. Enclosure by shrubs is not the same as enclosure by a brick wall.

When to Make Decisions

Therefore we have a whole series of decisions to make. These, which sometimes extend over many years, add up to the design of the house and garden, or home. Complete planning means sitting down with a plan of the lot and a program of our needs and desires before us, to make all of these decisions at once, in one continuous Operation Homeplan. This works best, because each decision affects all the others around it. Form and placement of house determine form and placement of garden areas; each room or separate space in house or garden is shaped by the others around it; the size and shape of every door, window, piece of furniture, tree or bush determines the size and shape of others around it; and so on.

It is quite true that we can find many charming homes which were not planned all at once, which have grown like Topsy over the years. Many of us feel that it is unnecessary, and perhaps a little unnatural, to plan so completely all at once. We have a feeling that a house and garden can and should grow, like a lovely scene in nature, over many years. Of course it should. But it will grow better from a plan than without one. If the plan has to grow with the garden its maturity will be delayed, and may never occur.

Our choice is really one of time; that is, of how long we want the planning process to take. A lovely home may well develop in 30 years without a master plan from the beginning. But all the thinking that would have gone into that plan will have been done through the years in a much more complex and wasteful way, often over and over again. The garden will grow by trial and error, and many plants and other elements will be tried, found wrong, and thrown away. The complete planning process builds on the accumulated experience of all the designers (amateur or professional) who have produced lovely gardens. This makes it possible to concentrate this trial and error pattern on paper within a few weeks or months. This complete plan can still be flexible enough to allow for changes or adjustments as work goes on.

After the House Is Built

We say that the normal process of building the house first, and then planning the garden, is apt to result in a considerable waste of space and bad connections between house and garden. And we say that it is therefore best to plan the whole lot at once as one series of indoor-outdoor rooms. However, we do not mean to imply that this idea applies only to the half million new detached homes being built every year. You may well say: How about the other thirty million families who are living in houses already built, some quite long ago? How are they going to get some of this smooth outdoor living, or these gorgeous vistas through the windows?

The idea of complete home planning is equally important to the owner of a raw lot ready for building, of a new house without landscaping, or of an older and more developed place which may need remodeling. The first principle of good planning is to examine everything that exists on the site. We must see how useful and how good- or bad-looking it is, and whether either its utility or its appearance might be improved by remodeling it or by putting it in some other location.

The owner of the new house on the undeveloped lot should sit down first with a plot plan which shows the size and shape of the lot, the floor plan of the house as it is located on the lot, and any changes in elevation which occur on the ground or between ground and floor level. He can then plot out the relations between indoors and outdoors as we have described them, making due allowance for personal preferences or problems peculiar to the house or site. This process makes it possible to design garden spaces which best

Complete home

planning for:

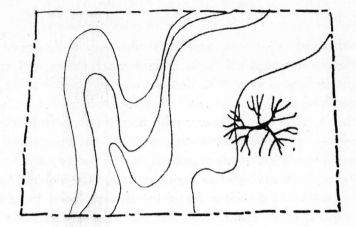

raw lot, or

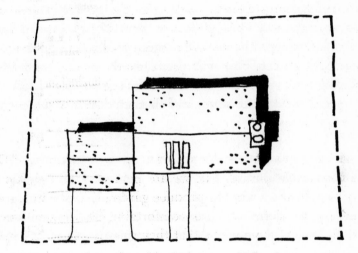

lot with house, or

lot with old house and garden

suit this particular house and lot. It also may well suggest small alterations in the house which will make it work much better with the garden. These might include a new door here or window there; a flight of steps made longer and shallower, a porch or stoop enlarged or extended; perhaps a garden terrace raised closer to the floor level of the house, or a section of house wall or roof extended some distance into the garden. This sort of idea makes it possible to produce not only useful and beautiful garden spaces, but better connections between these spaces and the rooms of the house.

The owner of the older house on the developed lot, if he is thinking of remodeling either house or garden, should also sit down with a plot plan as complete as the one just outlined. In addition, his plan should show all the principal features already existing in the garden: trees, shrubs, walks and terraces, steps and walls, pools, etc. Very often a careful bird's-eye examination of a developed home will suggest possibilities of re-orientation between house and garden that will prove much more beneficial than any small tinkering with either one alone. Careful remodeling of older homes will bring out special individual values and characteristics which cannot be duplicated in newer homes.

FIRST PRINCIPLE: UTILITY AND BEAUTY. "Design principles" is a formidable phrase, but we are beginning to develop some in spite of ourselves. First we want to produce garden spaces which are both useful and beautiful. By useful we mean comfortable, convenient, workable, or productive. By beautiful we mean that they give us pleasant, inspiring, or relaxing sensations. They may be warm or cool, calm or exciting, simple or picturesque, formal or informal, colorful, green, or structural. But if they are beautiful they will give us an experience which we will remember, and to which we will want to return. It is most important to combine the idea of utility with that of beauty. We may find gardens—such as a vegetable garden —which seem more useful than beautiful. We may find gardens—such as large estates—which seem more beautiful than useful. But the vegetable garden is most useful when it is most highly developed—with the best and most convenient arrangement and the healthiest plants—and a well developed vegetable garden has its own kind of beauty. On the other hand the estate garden is only beautiful when people are enjoying it, and it is useful to them because it gives them an experience which improves their sense of health and well-being.

SECOND PRINCIPLE: RELATIONS. Our second principle is that of the close connection between house and garden. This has been called the principle of *relations:* things which are seen together are most important to

Before

_____

After

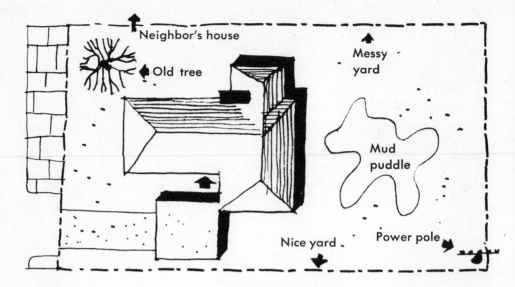

1. Plot plan & survey

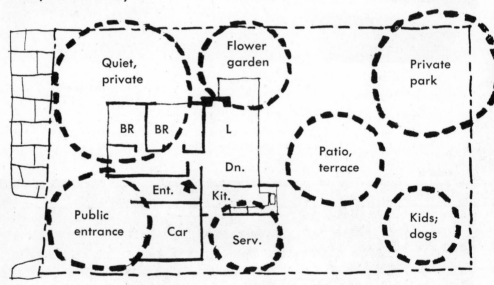

2. Relation study

3. The scale model

each other. Everything we add changes the quality of everything that is there already. Beginning with a bare lot, the first major change may be earthwork, and thereafter the construction of a house. Many of us have experienced the series of strong changes in apparent size of rooms and lot areas as these steps in grading and construction proceed. Thereafter we are familiar with the elimination of the bare and raw look of a new house by even the most ordinary type of landscaping. Following that we know how the garden (and therefore the house) changes year by year with the growth and change of plants. If finally after five or more years we suddenly realize that the plants are covering the house too much in the wrong places, and will have to be cut back or removed—then we know that there was something wrong in the original landscaping.

Although we are quite conscious of these major changes produced by grading, construction, planting, and growth, many of us are not so conscious of the change in quality produced by the introduction of each single piece of furniture, equipment, plant, or whatnot. This change is particularly difficult when these pieces come into the home one by one without conformance to an over-all plan. One by one they slip in, as gift or bargain, expedient or whim, until suddenly we realize that the place has become cluttered with unrelated objects which have destroyed its space and its quietude. Then we have to throw things out and start over again—with a plan if we are wise. With a plan we have learned to co-ordinate rather than to collect. That is, we have learned not to buy piece by piece, or plant by plant, and as each item is added we will see and feel the home growing toward the spatial picture we had in mind when we began.

How to Make a Plan

We begin with a plot plan as already mentioned, showing everything existing on the site, drawn accurately at a scale of 4, 8, or 16 ft. to the inch. Then we make a list of all the things we may want or need on the site, such as patio for outdoor living, space to dry clothes and burn trash, play area for small children, beds for cut flowers, shade in the summer, and so on. For each of these things we establish some rough size and shape, and also any special requirements (such as sun for cut flowers). We try to make a diagram of the proper relations between these elements and the house: patio off the living room, clothes-drying and trash disposal off the kitchen and laundry and out of sight of main living areas, play area where it can be supervised but still be out of the main garden picture, cut flowers in the sun but not too prominent unless we are exceptionally good gardeners, shade on the west from the afternoon sun (and sometimes on the east as well) and so on. Then we begin to make the actual plan, by sketching on tracing paper over our plot plan the various elements we want, in the rough size and shape they require, and in the right positions in relation to each other and the house.

This rough diagrammatic planning stage may take a little time or a lot of time, depending on how difficult your site, how exacting your requirements, and how well you can visualize on paper. If you have trouble with this, get some stakes and string and try to lay the areas and elements out on the ground. Then go back and put them on the plan. This working back and forth from the actual site to the plan on the drawing board is actually the way most professional landscape architects work. You may also try making a scale model, rough or finished depending on your skill. The important thing about studying a garden in model is to look at it from true eye level in the garden; not from above as in an airplane. This can be done by raising the model to eye level, by using a periscope as professional model-makers do, or by building a model-box with eye-level slits in the sides.

DETAILED DESIGN.   Once you have arrived at a rough diagrammatic plan which seems to solve all the problems, the detailed design begins. Now you have to make all the exact decisions as to what materials to use, what precise form and arrangement to give them, how much construction and how much planting are needed, how much screening or enclosure, how much shelter, how to enrich the garden with fine colors and textures and forms, how to make the drainage work, how to provide for irrigation, lighting, and so on.

These multiple decisions have to be made all together at about the same time, because each one has an effect upon most of the others. Materials, forms, and arrangements all go together; more construction means less planting, and therefore more initial outlay but less continuous maintenance (and vice versa); enclosure and shelter are the primary forming elements of garden spaces, giving them their principal character and quality; enrichment comes after these primary elements, not before (although they must make allowance for it); drainage and utilities must be established at the very beginning, before any more refined work is done.

The principal chapters of our book are devoted to these questions of detailed design. However, the primary fact that must be remembered is that all of these detailed decisions have to be made in connection with an over-all plan. Without a plan they are apt to get in each other's way. The garden then becomes a jumble or a collection of plants and furnishings, and all of its space and potential quality are lost.

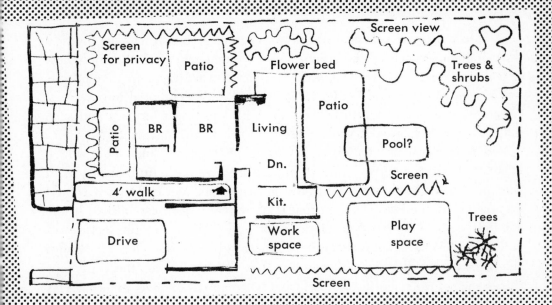

Functional study:

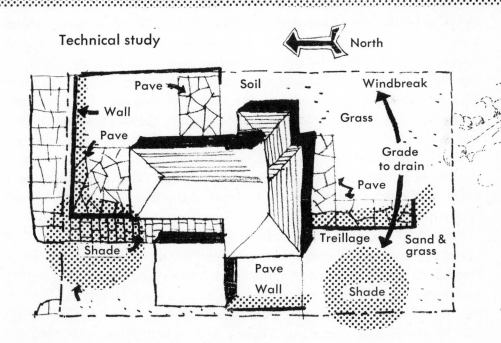

Technical study   ← North

Know-Why

Most of us are practical people who can carry out or manage physical development projects on the ground, once we understand all the know-how or technical questions involved. Most of us are also artistic or creative people, but it seems to be much harder for us to get at this potential in ourselves. Creativity is concerned with know-*why*—with knowing *why* such and such materials should be used in such and such forms and arrangements.

Perhaps because as a nation we tend to concentrate on know-*how*, which is apt to produce a narrow kind of practicality, we are a little uneasy with this question of know-why. It makes us suspicious. We feel that it should be inherent in the know-how, or that it has already been established in the printed pages of newspapers, periodicals, and books, or in the lectures of college professors. Yet it is precisely a concentration on knowing why things should be done in the way someone says they should be done (this is perhaps the essence of the scientific method) that has made us great as a nation. This pursuit of the WHY is as essential to the solution of small personal problems in house and garden as it is to the solution of large national problems of technology or politics. We will remain great and free just as long as we maintain our individual right to ask why we should do thus-and-so when someone in authority says we should.

The *why* of garden design is not easy to determine. The plan of a house is based on a multitude of practical functional and structural questions, which most home-owners examine quite thoroughly. They are therefore able to understand quite well why their houses are planned as they are. But from one simple diagrammatic plan of rooms and circulation and equipment many quite different-looking houses can be built. The roof may be gable, hip, butterfly, or flat, and have steep or shallow pitch; walls may have much glass and many doors, or few of either; materials may be masonry, wood or stucco. Similarly, the rooms may be closed up into tight boxes, or opened up into each other so that the house is just one large room. The variety in interior finish materials, colors, furnishings, and equipment is endless, as are their combinations.

Because of these multiple variations, many of us have a good deal of trouble in understanding *why* certain architects arrive at certain kinds of forms for houses (modern or traditional). Likewise many of us have trouble understanding why certain interior decorators produce certain kinds of interior arrangements (modern or traditional). Books of rules on house design and interior design are a dime a dozen, but most of them carefully avoid explaining *why* things should be thus-and-so. The principal virtue of serious modern design has been its concentration on this question of *why*. Perhaps we should say that modern design is virtuous as long as it concentrates on this question.

In the garden, functional and technical questions control the plan much less than in the house. The first problem in garden design is to find out just what problems of this sort exist, and to determine just how much control they may exert over the final form of the garden. A small garden which is to contain a swimming pool and a badminton court may have to conform exactly to their required shapes and sizes. Or a garden on a steep and irregular hillside may have to conform exactly in plan to possibilities of grading and terracing and the requirements of drainage.

But most gardens do not have such exacting requirements. We find usually that after all the functional diagrams and technical analyses have been made we still have the problem of determining just what form and arrangement to give these garden spaces, and just how to use materials in doing this. We are in somewhat the same position as the painter, with brush in hand, staring at a new blank canvas; or as the sculptor, hammer and chisel in hand, examining a new block of stone. In fact quite often we are faced with the question, not of where to place this or that activity, but of how to develop this garden space, for which there seems to be very little function, into something so pleasant and attractive that it becomes an asset rather than a liability.

This requires a search for discipline beyond functional or technical disciplines. The alternatives to discipline are whimsy, accident, or mysticism.

OLD RULES.   In the good old days this problem of how to shape the garden plan was made very simple for us. Dozens of garden handbooks, and every other issue of every house and garden magazine, gave us the simple lesson. Either you made it *formal*—or you made it *informal*.

If formal, you laid out a system of center lines through house and garden areas, strung oval areas of various sizes and shapes on these like beads, and then developed these areas with a whole system of neat little predesigned geometric walks and hedges, flower borders and tree roses, sundials, bird baths, benches and arbors. (Nothing is wrong with any of these elements but the way they were put together.)

If you made it informal you might use a similar system of center lines and ovals, developed with another packet of predesigned ungeometric wiggly walks and borders, pepper-and-salt shrub planting of fourteen kinds, and rustic structures. Of course to be really informal you had to abandon even the center lines, abandon geometry entirely, and rely on free curves and irregular arrangements. This was considered closer to nature, and therefore more beautiful.

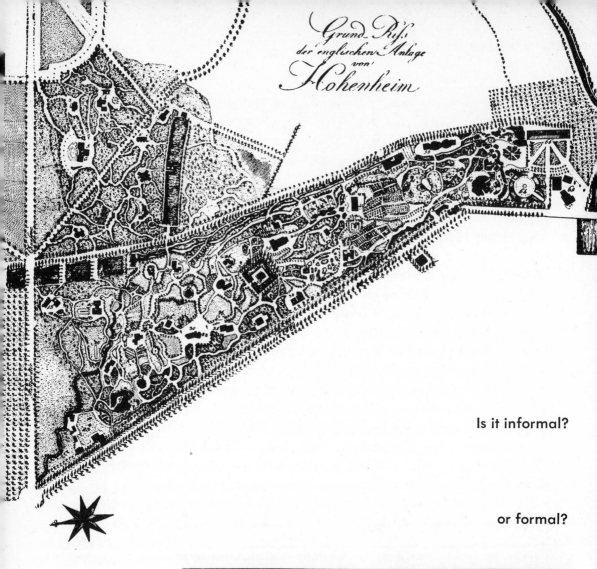

Grund-Riß der englischen Anlage von Hohenheim

Is it informal?

or formal?

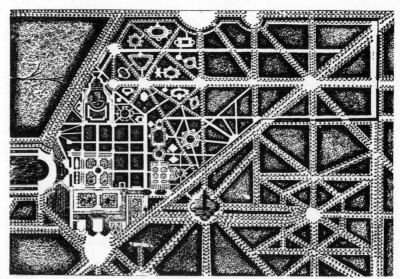

Thus we had two simple and infallible systems of design which made it unnecessary to ask the question *why?* One was based on a rigid and mechanical system of geometric patterns, the other on a respect for nature which tended to degenerate into an equally mechanical system of wiggly curves and scattered shrubs and trees.

NEW CONCEPTIONS. The proof of the pudding is always in the eating. There are many lovely gardens, both formal and informal, throughout our country. No one, this writer least of all, would want to destroy these, change them, or "modernize" them without very good reason. However the world does change (for the better), new ideas do develop from the new conditions of living in this changing world, and from these proceed new ways of looking at the physical world around us, and new conceptions of form and arrangement for that physical world.

These new conceptions may be constructive improvements or merely controversial. But as long as they concern themselves with the question *why*, they are healthy. We found that the old formal and informal patterns were no longer sources of inspiration and richness in the garden, but instead had become strait jackets which made all gardens mechanical imitations of each other. This was in truth regimentation, which was destroying individuality in garden design.

From this discovery began the search for better garden forms which has emerged more and more frequently in the pages of our house and garden magazines during the last twenty years. Some of these efforts have approached great landscape art; many have been merely trivial. But they have now brought us to a point at which we can examine garden forms for what they are. We can now decide whether they are good or bad solutions of a problem, irrespective of whether they are "modern" or "traditional."

The one great lesson of the many art controversies of this century is that art forms must be examined as physical and social realities, in terms of what they accomplish in the real physical world with real materials for real people with real problems. Any other basis for judgment, no matter how fancy its language, is quite irrelevant.

Significance of Plans

A plan on paper is an abstraction which is intended to control the development of real physical forms and actual arrangements on the ground. The connection between this paper abstraction and the final physical result

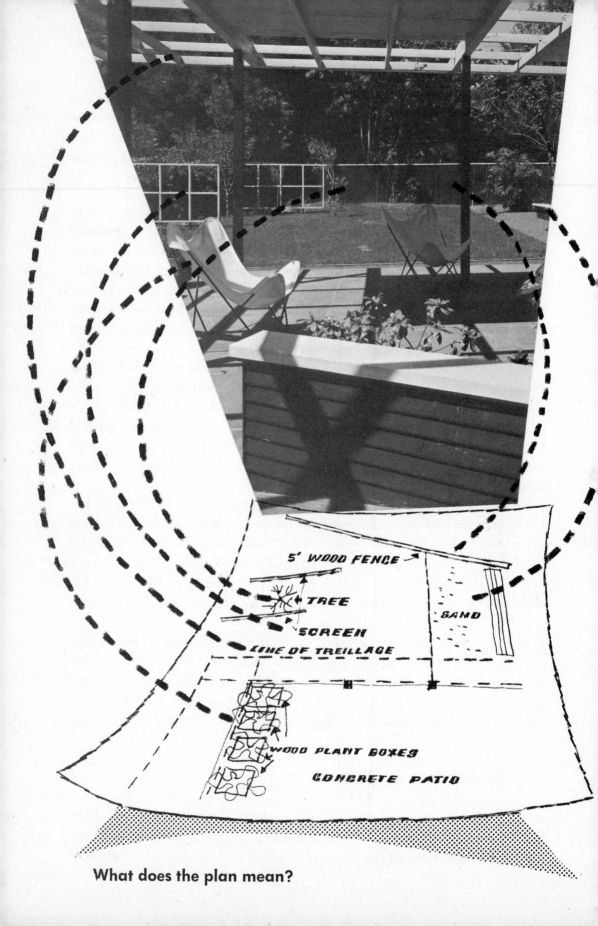

5' WOOD FENCE

TREE

SCREEN

LINE OF TREILLAGE

SAND

WOOD PLANT BOXES

CONCRETE PATIO

What does the plan mean?

is perhaps most difficult for the amateur to grasp. The extended periods of education (four to six years) and of experience in the field (five years or more) necessary to produce a professional who fully grasps this connection, indicate that it is a difficult skill to acquire. Nevertheless, this writer is convinced that if proper training in spatial visualization were given at the elementary and high school levels, many many more people would understand more fully this connection between scale drawing and full-size result. As it is, we must all do the best we can with the background and understanding that we have.

Perhaps the principle basic to the preparation of final plans is that *every line drawn on the plan must refer specifically to some real physical element on the ground.* The actual form and nature of this physical element must be clear in the mind of the planner when he draws the lines which refer to it. If we maintain this principle in practice, the pattern which the lines of the plan make on paper will have meaning; otherwise the plan is just an empty drawing, whether or not it may be pretty.

Any of us who have seen very many landscape plans may wonder how the planner arrives at those forms. A professional landscape architect has a background of study of the historical forms in his own art and in the allied fields of architecture, painting, sculpture, and others. Likewise, if he is interested in the world in which we live, he will have a good knowledge of contemporary developments in all these fields. He retains, of course, the privilege of selecting the forms he likes or dislikes from all this material. This gives him what is known as a *vocabulary of design forms.* Since landscape design is an art of visual forms, of things we see, it speaks with a vocabulary of such forms. Words are useful only to explain how and why it uses such forms.

The vocabulary which a particular designer develops from his background in historical and contemporary work must change and grow as he applies it to the solution of actual problems in the field. If his plans always look like the plans in the standard textbooks, he is not developing and learning from his experience. As we have seen, problems, sites, and materials vary in and within different parts of the country. It is the connection between these variable and changing problems (many of which are "new" because of the new ways of living which we are constantly developing) and the academic or abstract design vocabulary which produces a truly live landscape art.

I go into this much detail with regard to the forms used in professional design because anyone with sufficient interest, talent, time, and energy can go through the same process of design vocabulary development. The old "formal or informal" vocabulary system was too dry, mechanical, and restrictive. It did not allow for the production of forms variable enough to suit

variable problems and materials, and it tended to render imagination irrelevant. We are not interested in setting up a new system which would
also become dry and restrictive. We can, however, indicate the main elements in a vocabulary of landscape plan forms today, if we bear in mind the
principle that *all lines and forms on the plan must refer directly to real
materials on the ground.*

Most problems in garden design begin with a house on a lot which is small
enough to keep the garden always close to the house. Even on larger pieces of
land the tendency is to restrict developed garden areas in order to reduce
maintenance. The house is a geometric block, usually rectangular, although
often including other angular or circular forms. The lot may be flat and
rectangular, it may be odd in form, it may be more or less irregular in
topography, and it may have on it existing trees, rocks or other elements
which give it a more or less natural character.

The house, the lot and the materials which are to be used are the principal
sources of form in the garden. It is better to stick to simple forms that come
naturally from these existing facts than to introduce new forms that you
have seen elsewhere, unless you are quite sure how they should be used.

It is in the relation between house forms and land or site forms that the
old argument over formal versus informal still arises. Formal patterns are
architectural; that is, they are extensions of the house. Informal patterns are
intended to reflect the quality of the site, the land and the natural forms on
it, and still more of nature in general. Back of this lies the idea (quite correct)
that we need more contact with wild nature to maintain our health. However
if we let ourselves get trapped into an argument over whether the garden
forms should be architectural *or* natural, geometric *or* biologic, we make it
impossible to solve the problems. Gardens—usually—are places where architecture and nature meet and come together. Therefore they must include
forms which are *both* architectural and natural (formal and informal) in
order to become the best and most interesting gardens. This is true most of
the time, although one does quite often encounter special situations which
call for forms more purely architectural or natural.

BASIC VOCABULARY. On the basis of these principles and ideas, and
sufficient experience, one can outline a basic landscape design vocabulary
somewhat as follows:

First we have *rectangular patterns.* These are the simplest and most
natural for people to use in planning land development (simple geometry is
natural to people) and are usually direct projections from house forms. They
therefore make the most simple and direct means for integrating or connecting house and garden.

Next we have *angles* other than 90 degrees. Forty-five and 30-60 come naturally (too easily) from the standard triangles on the drawing board, but with an adjustable triangle one can draw all angles. Acute or obtuse angles may reflect angular forms in house or lot, or they may function to give direction to the eye and the foot going out of the house. Such angles can give a sense of space and motion impossible with right angles, if they are skillfully used.

Next we have *circular forms*—curves drawn from one radius point. These again may reflect forms in house or lot, or they may be introduced to add interest and richness to the garden pattern. Segments of circles are most useful in giving a sense of enclosure within the arc. In proper balance with straight-line forms they can give a very fine sense of equilibrium and stability.

Next we have the *free curve,* a form dear to the hearts of landscape gardeners and nature-lovers, and seldom found in architecture. This is a curving line with a constantly changing radius. Therefore it has no radius points and cannot be plotted geometrically (except perhaps in theory). This is the line which is drawn on paper with a soft pencil and a loose elbow, and is laid out on the ground with garden hose, rope, or a stick dragged in the hand. It is considered the line of beauty and the line of nature, and there is a subtle fascination in the thought that it cannot be reduced to any sort of rational discipline or control. In actual practice, though the form most used by unskilled designers, it is one of the most difficult forms to use successfully, because it takes most understanding of the relation between line and materials. Skillfully used, and carefully related to some geometric forms (including the house), it can bring maximum interest and richness to the garden.

These four are the simple basic forms from which all linear patterns in the garden are developed. One combination, which becomes a fifth basic pattern in use, is the *arc-and-tangent.* This is a continuous line which also changes direction often. But because it is made up of alternate straight lines and segments of circles, it can be constructed and plotted geometrically. It is a kind of geometric "free line" and might be called a compromise or a marriage between the idea of controlled geometry and the idea of the free curve.

Combined Patterns: From these five basic line patterns any number of combination patterns can be developed. It must be remembered that success in the use of any or all of these patterns depends entirely upon how carefully or skillfully they are used. They must develop naturally from the functional diagram of uses and areas which we called for first, and they must refer directly to the kinds of materials which are to be used in the garden.

Vocabulary

circular forms

William Aplin

arc-and-tangent

rectangular patterns

William Aplin; courtesy Sunset

free curve

Ernest Braun

Morley Baer

angles

We must also remember that actual precise physical lines in the garden can be produced only with refined structural materials—concrete, wood, cut masonry—or with carefully and persistently trimmed plant forms, such as hedges or grass edges. Many a landscape plan which shows fine line patterns on paper never produces them on the ground. This may be because the materials which are used are not sufficiently refined or processed to produce a consistent line on the ground, or because the maintenance is not sufficiently conscientious to preserve a line which was established at the beginning.

This leads us to a sixth basic landscape pattern, the *mass-and-void,* or *nonlinear.* This can be developed on paper only in rough diagrammatic form. Thereafter it must be worked out on the ground by arranging and rearranging the actual garden materials. It is the pattern of natural landscape elements: untrimmed plants, uncut rocks, irregular ground forms. These elements are not seen as linear forms, but as three-dimensional masses or branch-and-foliage structures. This is the pattern of all those landscape designers who are scornful of paper plans. It is the pattern of most Japanese and Chinese gardens, probably the most highly developed landscape traditions in the world.

For our problems and our way of life this nonlinear pattern represents a healthy means for bringing paper plans down to earth. It is generally most useful in combination with some of the linear plan patterns, because we usually find it necessary to use some precise elements, such as concrete paving or wood structures, in most gardens. Even these can of course be avoided by the use of such rough structural elements as flagstone, log sections, and split wood. Here again the choice and combination of patterns must come from the kind of house and lot problem which exists, as well as your desires. The more complex the combination of patterns and materials, the more skillfully and carefully must they be done to be successful.

Know-How

How about this know-how of design? How do we learn to put all of these complicated functions and patterns and materials together so as to produce a result that will look and feel harmonious, in addition to being useful? How do we produce design of quality?

The obvious answer, that quality design can be procured by going to a professsional landscape architect, only works for those of us who are able to pay the fees which a good designer deserves, and who live in areas where such services are available. Sincere professional practice involves selling only design and supervision services, with no commitments to any stocks of materials or labor payrolls. Such services are usually available only around the larger urban centers. In other sections design services may be provided by nurserymen or contractors. While often sincere and competent, these are apt to suffer from the distracting problems connected with selling materials and labor.

THE DESIGN PROCESS. Landscape design begins with:

1. The form which exists in house and lot
2. The technical problems house and lot may contain
3. The functions and uses which are desired by the residents
4. The physical properties of the materials to be used.

All of these have to be studied, analyzed, and understood thoroughly. Many, if not all, of the forms of the final design will come naturally and directly out of such a study.

When we find that we need more sources of form to complete the solution, or for greater interest, richness, and refinement, we explore the vocabulary which we have just outlined. The basis for understanding how to put together these various functions and patterns and materials is the development of a sense of form, or a feeling for the right relations and combinations. Some of us may be born with such a feeling so well developed that we never have to study to improve it. But most of us, including most professional designers, have to study to develop a sense of form, and we have to continue to study all of our lives in order to keep it in mature development. This study, as we have said, embraces the historical background of all fields of design, contemporary activity in all fields, and the general characteristics of the physical and social world which surrounds those activities. Nothing less is adequate to serious professional design. This no doubt seems like a large order to the simple reader who wants only to design his own garden and get it over with. We cannot expect him to enroll in this full curriculum. But we can suggest that he do some reading in these fields, as suggested in the bibliography, and perhaps undertake some part-time study in basic design, or any of the arts. From these he will begin to develop a basis for judging the quality of design.

Art critics or teachers will tell us that we begin with an idea based on certain purposes and goals. Using our imagination, within the framework of our memory and experience, we develop this idea into a form. This is developed with natural or man-made material, by analysis and the use of appropriate tools and processes. It will emphasize one or more of the art elements—line, shape, tone, color, texture, mass, space; will be arranged according to the art principles—rhythm, balance, emphasis; and will be so organized by proportion as to produce harmony, which is a careful relation-

1

2

Baldinger garden

Photos by Tom Burns Jr.

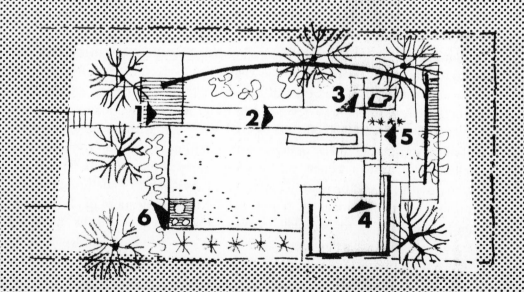

This garden is an excellent example of the disciplined development of quality garden space from a very bare and ordinary beginning. It concentrates on the production of a refined sense of enclosure or volume, and in addition, on a richness in form and texture in the enclosing elements. Rhythm exists in the continuity of fence structure, balance in the arrangement of fence, tree, and paving forms, and emphasis in the placement of the sculpture. The proportions and scale of these combined forms are highly refined, and the unity of fence and sculptural forms includes a considerable variety in wood detail, paving pattern, and planting. The entire garden combines qualities of repose and movement—neither dominates; rather they are in balance.

ship between unity and variety. This form should have vitality, and an effect of either repose or liveliness.

Thus we put together functions and patterns and materials in the garden according to rhythm, balance and emphasis.

Rhythm is repetition of elements—a row of trees, a flight of stairs, a succession of similar rocks—which may be regular or irregular.

Balance means having elements of similar importance—size or form or color or interest—placed carefully at two or more points in composition.

Emphasis means bringing forward certain elements, such as a pool, a bird bath, a flowering tree, or a rose bed—to concentrate interest on them.

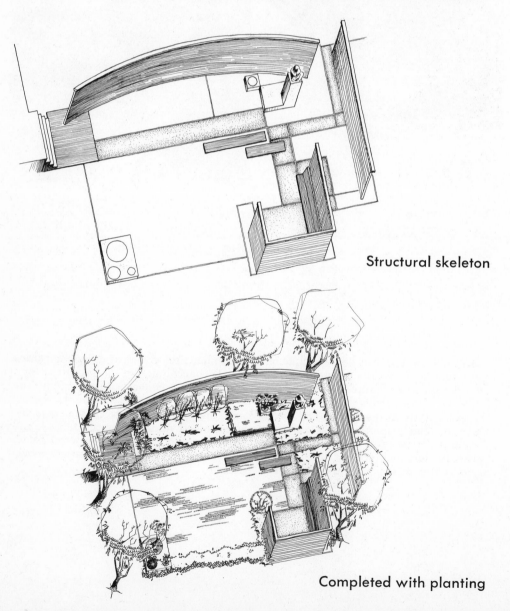

Structural skeleton

Completed with planting

This arrangement is organized by *proportion*, which is the quantity relation between various forms, materials, solid elements, and open spaces. It is this proportion which primarily determines the success of your garden scheme. Thus at one place a large paved terrace and a small lawn may be in good proportion, while at another place the terrace should be small and the lawn large. But we would almost never make both equal in size. Small "busy" elements (such as flower beds, lily pools, sculpture) need large simple elements (hedges, walls, lawns) around them to quiet them down. A few vertical forms need to be balanced with many horizontal elements, or vice versa. This proportioning of the various elements in the garden is the process by which it is continuously refined down to a serious work of art.

One factor of great importance in this process is *scale*. In other words, how big or small does the garden feel? How open or closed? If we can make it feel bigger and more open, or richer and more interesting than it was in the beginning, we feel successful. This has to do not only with the shapes and sizes of areas, but also with the details of planting and construction. Wide boards in a fence will make the adjoining space feel smaller; narrow boards, larger. A preponderance of large leaves will also shrink space, while small foliage will make it feel larger. Dark strong colors will reduce apparent space, while light clear colors will enlarge it.

A harmonious combination of unity with variety can result from this proportioning process. If unity is a garden planted with only one kind of shrub throughout, and if variety is a garden planted with one each of two hundred kinds of shrubs, then clearly the harmonious garden will have more than one but fewer than two hundred kinds. Moreover it will not have the same numbers of each kind, but rather many of some (for background) and few of others (for emphasis).

This is an extremely sketchy outline of the considerations leading to design quality. There is, of course, no limit to the depth and thoroughness with which they can be explored. But they exist and are important in every design process, no matter how amateur or how occasional. By this we mean that every time you make a decision about what to put into, or take out of, your garden or house you are making a design decision which involves rhythm and proportion and harmony. This should be rooted as firmly as possible in understanding of needs for space, the properties of garden materials, the desires of all the family, and the local conditions. Together these abstract and realistic factors can produce great design in many gardens.

An example herewith, and the case studies in Chapter 4, should illustrate the practical development of these ideas.

4. Case Studies

The gardens in this chapter have been carefully selected to illustrate typical problems. Small urban gardens and larger suburban places have been included, but no large or showy estates. We have endeavored to show the varying possibilities of flat, sloping, and steep sites, and to include remodeled older gardens as well as new properties. There are gardens with views outside their boundaries as well as gardens which must be self-sufficient; gardens for adults and gardens for families with children. The presentation will also include the solution of specific technical problems, such as soil, drainage, wind or sun, which the site may present.

In all cases the emphasis is on a spatial framework which will house general and specific activities and functions with flexibility to adjust to changes over the years. We feel that family life is seldom static, that major changes occur in it every five to seven years when it includes children, and that therefore the garden must be designed as a generous and beautiful framework enclosing and housing this rich life. It must provide a background with color and interest sufficient to enliven the family's work and play without being so strident as to frustrate or confuse. We are conscious always of the tremendous variability inherent in detailed landscape design—private sites and problems are always special and individual, never repetitive except in some details. Materials available have a great range and variety. The unified design concepts developed to solve these problems with these materials can have similar variability, comparable to the variety of painting or sculpture.

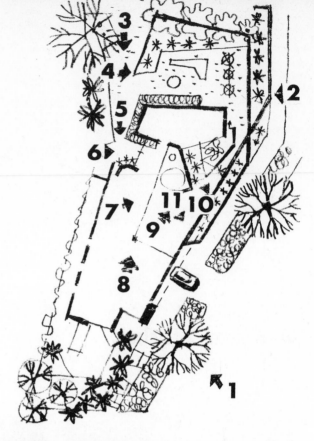

THORMIN

Anthony Thormin, Architect
Julius Shulman, Photographer

1	2
3	4

One of the most successful collaborations between architect and landscape architect in our experience. House took full advantage of a steep, narrow corner lot. Entrance at the high end, directly on main floor elevation, carefully designed as a graceful, hospitable space leading from the sidewalk to the concealed front door. Through this glass door one looks directly across the entry hall into a corner of the main patio. Paving patterns of tile and colored rough concrete flow through the entry and culminate in a sculptured pool and planter backed by a low tile wall. Interesting planting is concentrated behind this, leaving most of the small patio open paved living space, extending the living and dining rooms. The master bedroom also opens into this patio, through a more private entrance. In front of the house and to the left of the entrance is a fair-sized garden area with raised beds for growing flowers and small fruits.

An additional small yard in the rear, at the low end of the lot, was designed as additional recreation area, including a possible small pool. This area is one story below the living floor, accessible from it and from the street.

1. House from side street—rear and garage entries show. A patterned fence screens rear yard. House wall of plywood extends to enclose patio above concrete block retaining walls. Plants include evergreen magnolia, Chinese photinia, dusty miller, English ivy, sweetgum, lemon gum.

2. From side street nearer corner—patterned screen connects bedroom patio with front garden. Plants include lemon gum, dracaena palm, English ivy, citrus varieties.

3. Front entrance from sidewalk: Plants include giant bamboo and California sycamore to right.

4. The garden: Plants include German iris, roses, tulips, Meyer lemons and other citrus, persimmon.

5. Entry garden: Screen of combed plywood; plants include Meyer lemons, Japanese maple, Woodwardia fern, giant bamboo, dwarf windmill palm, star jasmine.

6. Through the entry hall: cement tile on chimney and walk; plants include Woodwardia fern, fiddle-leaf fig, horsetail, rice paper, flowering pineapple.

7. Patio from living room.

8. Indoors-outdoors: Living-room patio.

5 | 6
7

8

Thormin

9. The patio.
10. Bedroom patio.
11. Storage wall and sink in patio.

Small house, owner-built; sloping lot. Entry and patio on levels established with the house by grading at each side of the house rectangle. The garden slopes away on the downhill side of the house, preserving the valley view.

Repetition of circle as a design unit in paving pads to major terrace; permanent bench reinforces circular pattern and directs the view from the patio.

2

BRENNAN
Henry Hill, Architect
Morley Baer, Photographer

1

Remodeling of a typical stucco cottage on a narrow corner lot. Small garden spaces include: Front lawn—walk widened and patterned, planting simplified and made more orderly. Entrance patio already enclosed, like the rest of the yard, with a 5-ft. stucco wall. Rich and interesting entry combined with auxiliary living space on the cool side of the house. Dining terrace developed from narrow passage space by raising level, screening one side and railing the other. Interesting semi-shade planting at rear of passage. Rear patio developed as a unified living space with sun and shade. Floor combines paving and lawn; screen baffles gate to street; large bench is provided for sprawling. Shelter designed to create lower and more intimate ceiling.

1. View within entry garden. Trellis and low divider of redwood; plants include African iris, rice paper, papyrus, New Zealand flax.

2. Dining terrace created by raising level to that of house floor. Screen of celluloid-on-wire in redwood frame above existing stucco wall. Sacred bamboo, honey bush and bugleweed in foreground.

3. View from dining terrace back into entrance garden showing sculptural concrete blocks and metal bowl at left.

4. Screen around service entrance. Camellia, azalea, *Hardenbergia*.

5. Rear patio, showing wide bench, suspended shelter and translucent screen (same detail as other photos). Wistaria on trellis.

6. Rear patio, showing bench, translucent screen at street gate, and existing stucco wall. Wistaria on arbor, papyrus against screen, jacaranda in lawn of *dichondra* which requires no mowing.

RICH

Joseph Johnson, Architect
William Aplin, Photographer

1

William Aplin; courtesy Sunset

2

3

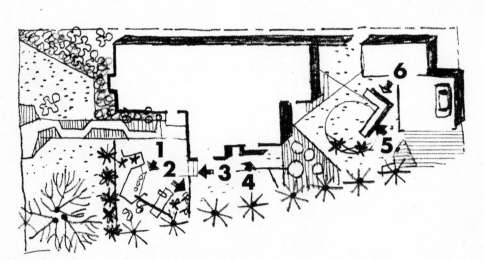

4

5

6

STAFFORD

Richard J. Neutra, Architect
Ernest Braun, Photographer

1

2   3

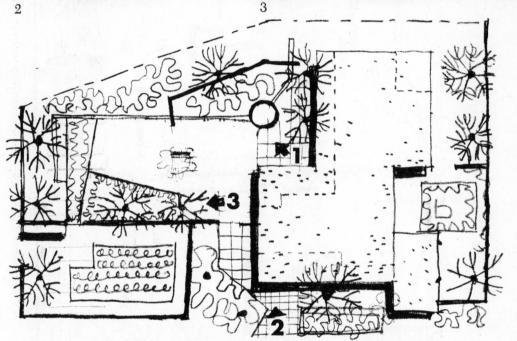

Site—A suburban corner lot, part of an old prune orchard.

Problems or conditions: Readjustment of boundary and access to neighboring house occupied by a relative. Owners have dogs; no children. Therefore: (1) no lawn, (2) all plantings in raised or bordered beds to help train dogs to stay out of planted areas. Owners like to garden; wanted space for raising flowers and bulbs in main garden; also special vegetable garden with tool storage area and access for trucks with soil, manure, etc. Favorite color: yellow. View from dining room to include salad and herb growing area. Service area and dog run required; also truck access to a firewood storage area.

Fence and trellis are connected to house to provide privacy from neighboring house, back up pool, and extend wall material out into garden.

Redwood curbs surrounding plant beds are of various weights and heights, depending on designer's ideas of where strength, contrast, width, slimness or "up or downness" was needed.

Fence between main garden and vegetable garden is interesting. The two different functions of total separation and partial separation are served by change in spacing of the fence material, a device which preserves unity.

Use of macadam as a garden surface has been very successful.

Angular lines, forced by relation to neighboring property, are balanced to create design movements more exciting than rectangular lines. Circular forms like the pool seem to work well in such an angular frame.

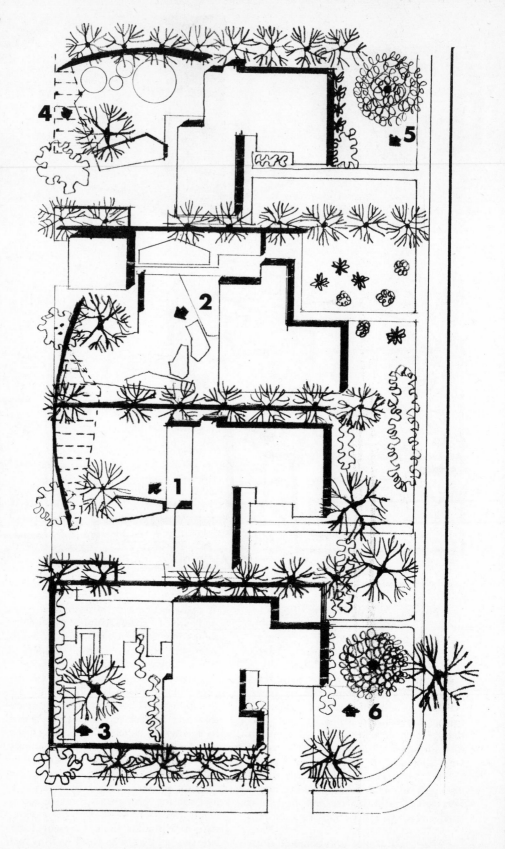

MEADOWLARK PARK

Edward H. Fickett, Architect
Evans Slater, Photographer

1

Four model houses for a tract of 1100 units in the $15,000 price bracket. Architectural design stressed indoor-outdoor living. Gardens were developed to demonstrate the variety of possibilities in these average size yards. Paving patterns in brick, concrete and asphaltic concrete; fences of plywood and 1 x 1 redwood; three-dimensional trellis for grapes and berries; shelters and sandboxes; planting designed to create space in front and rear yards as well as to set off the houses. Careful analysis was made of the relations of all door and window openings to the space outside and to the neighbors. Screening provided where needed.

The design of the gardens endeavored to create a unified neighborly feeling by the repetition of two typical fence details and the extension of arbors between gardens. At the same time the design endeavored to individualize the gardens by providing a different kind or pattern of paving and planting in each.

1. Fencing of redwood 1 x 1's set vertically and stained, and painted weatherproof plywood. Arbor posts redwood, top Douglas fir, all painted.

2. Sandbox and dividing trellis in foreground.

3. Sandbox, existing fig tree, brick paving, trellis for grapes and berries.

2

3

4. Pebbly concrete circles, structure of 1 x 1 fence.

5. Entrance garden, pfitzers and twisted junipers, Siberian Elms, sandankewa.

6. House fronts, existing oak and acacia to right, evergreen mock orange to left.

1

2

3

BOLLES

John Bolles, Architect
Esther Born, Photographer (1)
M. Halberstadt, Photographer (2 and 3)

Typical problem of the compact boxy house set up 18 in. and more above a flat lot falling away somewhat to the rear. Connection with the garden solved by building up L-shaped terrace connecting house with shelter at side of carport, and broad steps leading down to main garden. Curved screens and row of pipe columns with trellis establish structural extension of house into garden. Spatial organization of garden, open lawn, wading pool, badminton court and play yard is established by these elements.

1. From lawn back toward house. Terrace of redwood with surfacing of fine crushed red rock.

2. From badminton court toward carport shelter.

3. From living terrace toward garden. Weeping willow to right existed; Lombardy poplars in rear were planted.

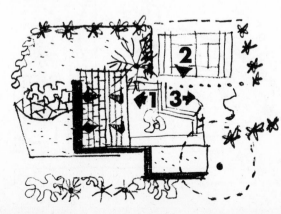

SLATER
Evans Slater, Photographer

1

2

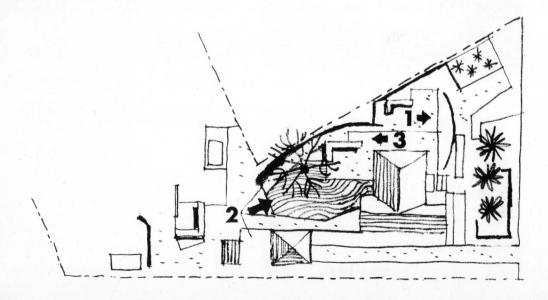

A triangular lot, somewhat higher at the rear, next to a public park. To this triangle was added a good-sized rectangle, to which the triangle provides the only access. The house was a typical small tract structure. The garden is designed to give maximum privacy and livability, in order to enlarge the house. Living room has since been remodeled by Richard Jampol, architect, to give direct access to patio by means of a sliding glass wall. Brick and redwood are used in curved and straight-line forms to give rich and flexible enclosure. Colored and pebbly concrete, small pool with pedestal, and textured planting increase interest and richness.

1. Across patio toward pool, showing comfortable broad benches.

2. From rear garden toward patio, showing spacious quality of this fairly small garden.

3. From patio toward rear garden, showing fine existing trees.

3

WOHLSTETTER

Josef Van der Kar, Architect
Julius Shulman, Photographer (1-5)
Evans Slater, Photographer (6 and 7)

A hillside house, with a lovely view over a wooded valley. Entrance from the uphill side directly into the main living floor. Balcony cantilevered from this floor overlooks the main garden terrace, one story down, which is entered from the downstairs playroom and guest room. This terrace is developed in fanciful patterns of concrete paving and sculptured earth ridges planted with dichondra. A large metal bowl provides a pool which is planted with horsetails.
1. House from neighboring vegetable garden.
2. Guest terrace with mound separation.
3. Guest terrace from playroom.
4. Living balcony.

1

2

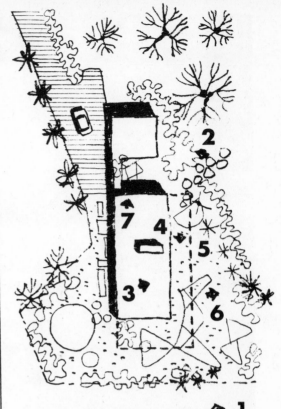

2

7 4

5

3

6

1

3

3

4

5

Wohlstetter

5. Main garden terrace.
6. Pool on main terrace.
7. Daughter's bedroom garden, showing pool, with sculpture by Leon Saulter.

6

7

HELLMAN

Campbell & Wong, Architects
Morley Baer, Photographer

1

Problem: Remodel 75 year old house and garden. Provide level garden usable for entertaining with good relationship to living room.

The old garden lacked this good relationship to living room. (Paved area was depressed 3. ft., and entrance to it through little octagonal hall was tight.) The back part of garden sloped uncomfortably. Small flowering plum was only existing plant worth saving. Solution was to bridge over old paved area at living room level and extend the same level by excavating and hauling away dirt and building retaining wall at back. Bridge is built of wood, and excavated area is exposed aggregate concrete paving. Linear pattern of wood decking accentuates depth of garden. House post module is recognized in order to give relief and rhythm to deck members, and to carry pattern into concrete area. Raised planting beds add interest and control to planting spaces.

1. View from living room to back of garden. To the left is kitchen door with small enclosed service area. In background is retaining wall necessitated by excavation. This wall, which is concrete, is covered with redwood bark. Basically the whole house and garden is wood: wood shingles, wood deck, wood fences, and wood posts. Redwood, which is soft and has a fine texture, provides a definite contrast and a quiet receding mass at the end of this comparatively short garden. It also provides a sympathetic surface over which to train fuchsias.

2. Plant boxes in which seasonal foliage or flowering plants are placed. Purpose: to end stairway fence short of the glass and provide screening of the stairway from the living room.

3. View at back of garden looking toward living room. Roof and trellis provide overhead protection and privacy from neighbors, and a transition space between house proper and garden proper. Plum at left of photo was existing. Low fence at left encloses service stairway which goes under living room to garage and street. Master bedroom has balcony upper left.

2

3

HARRIS

House and swimming pool design by Gene
Julius Shulman, Photographer (1-4)
William Aplin, Photographer (5-7)

Interesting two-story modern house built across a small valley, with an idyllic view down into oaks and sycamores. Entrance from parking bay down ramp past sculptural pools. Main garden a bowl of dichondra and sand, framed by slate terrace, blacktop walks, and badminton area all given plastic form. Stairway through planted rockwork connects house to carport.

1. House and slate terrace from carport. Tree is California live oak.

2. House from street. Plants include honey bush, leatherleaf, golden bamboo, duranta, California sycamore, wild strawberry.

3. House and main garden from entry. Plants include weeping pittosporum, rhubarb, blue ice plant, New Zealand flax, purple sand cherry.

4. Toward house from badminton area. Purple magnolia in foreground.

2

3

2

4

1

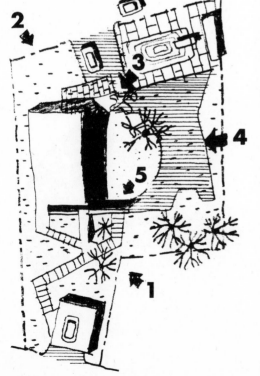

Harris

5. Stairs of redwood and square brick pavers to carport.
6, 7. Details of stairs, rockwork and planting.

5

6

7

William Aplin; courtesy Sunset

FRIMKESS

Kemper Nomland Jr., Architect
Julius Shulman, Photographer

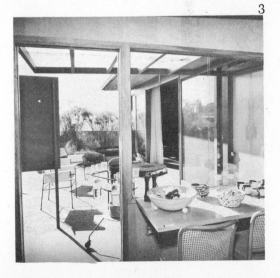

New home on very steep lot—25 ft. fall in 75—required careful integration of house and garden design to produce maximum living space. Main patio retained between house and hillside; entry screened from patio with curved screen. Paving, retaining walls, fountain and base combined into sculptural ensemble. Connection to street by steps and stepped ramps to carport. Planting below house (20 ft. down) is designed to give a sense of security, framing the view with a pattern of branching at and above eye level, and vegetation below.

Photographs are all views into patio, showing close relation to house. Planting includes papyrus, rice paper, jacaranda.

RANGELL
Julius Shulman, Photographer

1

Boxy two-story stucco house on flat lot with steep slope at rear. Garden designed to create maximum outdoor living space, tying house to site and to mountain view north from rear garden. Front yard developed to provide auto turn and extra parking. Entrance patio (on warm west side) enclosed within ell of house by circular wood screen. In rear, long arbor connects living room and garden; triangular arbor emphasizes view. Paving patterns feed irregularly out into green. Freeform screen gives touch of fantasy. Grove of thin lemon gums on north side frames view and balances arbor.

1. Triangular arbor. African iris and rubber tree in foreground.

2. South side rear garden showing freeform screen, which is stained red. Ground cover wild strawberry. Other plants include fern pine, bottle brush and fatshedern.

3. View down long arbor. Star jasmine and jacaranda in foreground.

2

3

4

4. North from triangular arbor. Pebbly concrete walk connecting with play area of dry decomposed granite. Plants include Carolina jessamine, ice plant, African iris, African box, lemon gum, bushy blue gum, papyrus.

5. View from street northwest, showing drive, turn, parking space and entrance patio screen. Trees at left are Brazilian pepper; tree at right is scarlet gum. Foreground plants include New Zealand flax, helichrysum, and striped grass.

5

6. House from street southwest *after*. Parking space to left, entrance patio screen to right. Plants include New Zealand flax, tipu tree, castor bean, white birch, Algerian ivy.
6a. House from street *before*.

6

7. Across entrance patio from front door. Plants include Carolina jessamine, rice paper, bird-of-paradise, gazania, rhubarb, tipu tree, Australian cherry left rear, bottle brush rear outside screen.

8. Detail of concrete pattern north side rear garden. Ice plant ground cover. Plants include leather leaf, New Zealand flax, honey bush, lemon gum. Bushy blue gum beyond neighbor's wall.

7

Rangell

ROSENBERG

Campbell & Wong, Architects
Morley Baer, Photographer

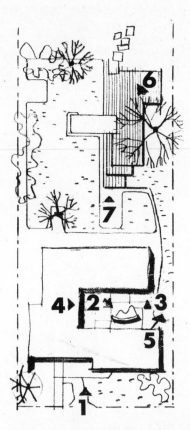

Site: City lot rising gently to a levee in back and then dropping to the canal. View across levee was not good, so levee top is used for cut flower and vegetable garden and is screened from main garden by 4-ft. fence.

Existing weeping willow, which provides very necessary summer shade, made possible the development of the main usable paved area under this tree and allowed the grass area to extend up close to the living and dining room windows, thereby reducing the amount of reflected light and heat.

Arrangement of house (bedrooms in a wing near the street and the living room, dining room and kitchen in a rear wing) provides an interior court between living room, bedrooms and connecting hallway.

2. Detail of patio pool. Water enters pool through small copper tubes piercing tile wall. Concrete coping has rubbed finish with gray integral color. Indentation in vertical face of coping is to lighten its general appearance, separate it from the paving, and bring out the form by providing an additional surface.

3. Reverse of No. 4. Master bedroom at left, hall in background, and living room at right. All open into this patio or court.

4. View from hall which connects living room on left and bedrooms on right side of garden court. Court features fountain and pool, rich planting, and decorative fence in background on the lot line. Young flowering cherry will in time provide more overhead interest.

(Fence panel designs by Asa Hanamoto of Eckbo, Royston & Williams.)

Paving of patio is of alternating areas of gray exposed aggregate concrete and tan smooth concrete.

2

3

4

5

terrace and house allows grass to penetrate into this space, reducing glare and heat. Terrace is tan concrete. House is natural cedar siding. Wood flower beds with white trim integrate house and garden by material and form repetition, and give linear direction, thereby creating spaces within the larger space of the garden.

7. View opposite No. 6, looking from house to main outdoor living under willow. Levee is in the background. It was graded down 2 ft. to provide fill and decrease total vertical height to a more comfortable degree. Louver fence on top of levee shields cut flowers and vegetables and screens view of houses across the canal in back. Lath house in right hand corner is for starting young seedlings. Neighbor to the right has a tall aviary (center, right).

Width and flow of steps is important for comfortable access and to offset vertical lines of weeping willow. Linear contrast and repetition is provided also by fence, bulkhead, and flower box.

Concrete of lower level and steps is gray exposed aggregate—again to reduce glare in house and provide richer texture than smooth concrete.

5. Detail of fence on property line at end of garden court. Frame is painted white; pierced panels of tempered Masonite are painted gold and the background panels are light brown and gold. Wild strawberry ground cover; red-leaved New Zealand flax.

6. Taken from main living terrace under weeping willow tree. Grade of tree allowed terrace level to be raised above house floor. Separation of living

6

NISHI

Kazumi Adachi, Dike Nagano, and Hideo Takeyama, Architects
Julius Shulman, Photographer (1-3)
Evans Slater, Photographer (4-8)

Refined, elegant modern house, large flat lot. House incorporated good-sized patio and ornamental pool in its architectural framework. Front yard primarily in paving for auto turning and parking, surrounded by ornamental patterns of planting, rocks, and low walls. Rear garden designed as a fanciful extension of the house, in patterns of dry paving with redwood headers, low redwood walls, free-standing trellis, raised lounging platform, and a sculptured-masonry enclosing wall. South of the house a private fenced-in garden off the bedrooms is planned in a closely interlocked pattern of dry paving and low patterns of colorful plants: *Aster frikarti,* calla lilies, acanthus, Martha Washington geraniums, arctotis, torch lilies, daylilies, rhubarb, azaleas, sago palm, lily of the valley tree.

1. Entrance, showing auto parking space.

2. Entry court.

3. Patio pool from bedroom.

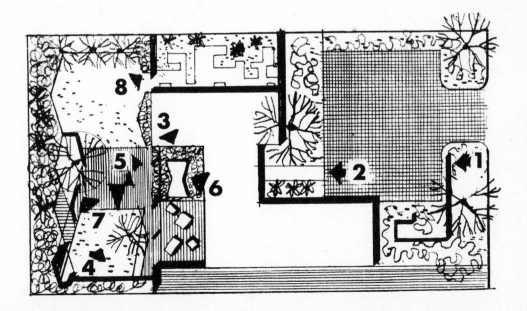

Nishi

4. Rear garden toward house.
5. Pool planting: twisted juniper, African iris, sacred bamboo, Japanese maple, papyrus.
6. Pool from terrace.
7. Lounging platform.
8. Bedroom garden.

7

8

5. Foundations

Gardens have foundations even as houses. The earth which is your lot is not only the floor of your block of potential living space, it is also the foundation which will support the house and all other structures, and the soil in which half of each and every plant in the garden will live and grow, or die.

Problems connected with the handling and treatment of this earth must be thought of first, because you will never have as good a chance to think of them again.

These problems are often expensive and difficult. There is a widespread tendency to postpone them or slough them off as though they weren't really necessary. This only aggravates them, or may even make them completely insoluble. Labor and money put into these garden foundations is most important and essential. Even though little or nothing may show above ground when they are completed, even though you may have to defer some of the garden till later in order to do them, it is best to do them first. This is literally like putting money in the bank. It saves endless expense and trouble later on.

These foundation problems are concerned with grading, drainage, soil conditioning, and utilities. These problems must all be solved together, and all of them are found in every garden.

Grading is any change in the slope of the ground, no matter how slight.

Drainage is the movement of water over the surface of the ground, and below the surface between the particles of earth.

Soil conditioning is the preparation of soil for planting.

Utilities are the pipelines—water, gas, electrical, and sewer—which lie or must be installed below the surface of the ground as traps for the unwary pick or shovel.

Grading

Grading involves excavating and filling. This is usually done to provide approximately level areas for construction or outdoor living, or ramps for access to such areas. It may also be done for more specialized purposes: to control erosion, excavate pools, build protective berms or ridges, lay out golf greens, or just improve the form of a piece of land. Grading is done with a wide range of tools, from the basic pick, shovel, and rake through all sizes of tractors and bulldozers to giant power shovels, carry-alls and prime movers. Usually only the smaller tools are needed on residential properties. The great and simple potential of grading for maximum improvement of the utility and beauty of land is often overlooked or evaded because of prejudice.

Soils and earthwork techniques vary throughout the country, but certain principles are basic to all regions. Earth consists of an aggregation of small particles, derived from the decomposition of rock and organic materials. In composition it may vary from the slight adhesive qualities of sand to the strong adhesive qualities of clay. It has always an original rock base, and at times this comes to the surface in more or less dominant quantities.

Because of its composition as an aggregation of particles, earth can seldom be made to hold a very steep slope. Therefore its forms take on a stable pyramidal quality. This is based on the "angle of repose," the slope a given pile of dirt will assume without structural retention. Sand has the lowest angle of repose, rock the highest. Most soils fall between them. Solid rock can be cut to a vertical cliff, or nearly so, but weathered particles will then begin to collect at its base. Normal maximum angles for ordinary soil are one vertical to one horizontal (1:1) for cut slopes, and 1:2 for fill slopes. Cut slopes are excavated; fill slopes are loose dirt piled up, or pushed over a slope. Slopes can of course be made flatter than these angles, or steeper with retaining walls or other structural assistance (cribbing, Guniting, straw and wire, or surfacing with rock, blocks, or brick).

The making of a cut or a fill is only the beginning of the necessary operation. It is the failure of excavators and graders to follow through with the necessary finishing touches that has given grading a black eye in many parts of our country. A newly cut or filled slope will not long remain smooth and stable without certain essential control measures. First, surface water from above must not be allowed to run over the slope. If it does, the slope will erode and wash away. This surface water can be diverted from the top of the slope with berms or ditches. Thereafter drainage facilities should be provided to carry it to the nearest street, storm drain, or natural watercourse.

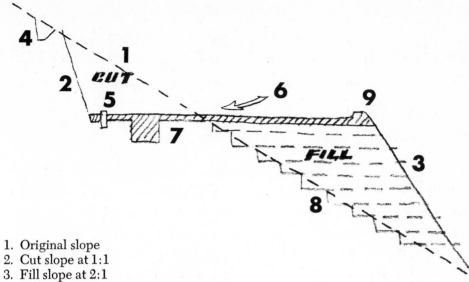

1. Original slope
2. Cut slope at 1:1
3. Fill slope at 2:1
4. Diversion ditch to keep water off cut
5. Retaining wall to hold topsoil and catch slough from cut
6. Drain toward cut
7. Topsoil: 6 in. for lawns, 18 in. for flowers, 2 ft. for shrubs, 3 ft. for trees
8. Original slope benched to receive fill
9. Built-up berm to control runoff

Grading

Grading creates scars like these.

Becsky

COVERING THE SURFACE. Once slopes and drainage controls have been established, all bare ground surfaces should be covered as rapidly as possible. This coverage can be of either planting or paving. Its purpose is to protect the surface from the direct impact of rain and wind, and also to minimize the slow decomposition and crumbling produced by chemical reaction with the atmosphere. Cut slopes which are too hard or sterile for direct planting can be screened or covered with vines, shrubs, or trees, planted above or below. Nature does not allow bare ground to remain undisturbed. She will cover it with volunteer grasses and weeds (although perhaps not soon enough to prevent erosion) or, as in arid regions, she will subject it to heavy erosion. (The principles and practices developed by the Soil Conservation Service of the U.S. Dept. of Agriculture are applicable to the control of all types of disturbed ground.)

GRADING ORDINANCES. Few communities escape heavy concentrations of rainfall. When this happens, badly made cuts and fills in hillside residential areas wash out, doing tremendous damage. As a result of such experiences, many cities now have in operation stringent and efficiently written grading control ordinances. Such control is basic to the safety and stability of the results of every grading operation. Typically it may require the submission of plans and specifications, securing of a permit and regular inspection of all grading operations except: excavations not over 5 ft. deep vertically; fills of not over 5 cu. yd. of material, or not over 3 ft. deep vertically at the deepest point, or with no slope greater than 1:5, vertical to horizontal.

The ordinance may establish maximum cut and fill slopes and drainage controls as above. In addition it should have an important section titled: "Compaction of Fills." All fills intended to support buildings or structures should be made to a minimum 90 per cent compaction. Compaction of other fills need not be required except where necessary as a safety measure to aid in preventing the saturation, slipping, or erosion of the fill. Where compaction is required, the percentage depends upon the particular circumstances and type of fill.

COMPACTION. The steps in compaction include but are not limited to the following:

1. Preparation of the natural ground surface by removing topsoil and vegetation and by compacting the fill upon a series of terraces
2. Control of moisture content of material used for the fill
3. Limitation on the use of various kinds of materials

Scars can be healed like this.

Before

Three-year planting of kudzu on severely gullied area, made by the Soil Conservation Service of the U.S. Department of Agriculture in Hall County, Ga.

After

Grading can produce terraced gardens like this.

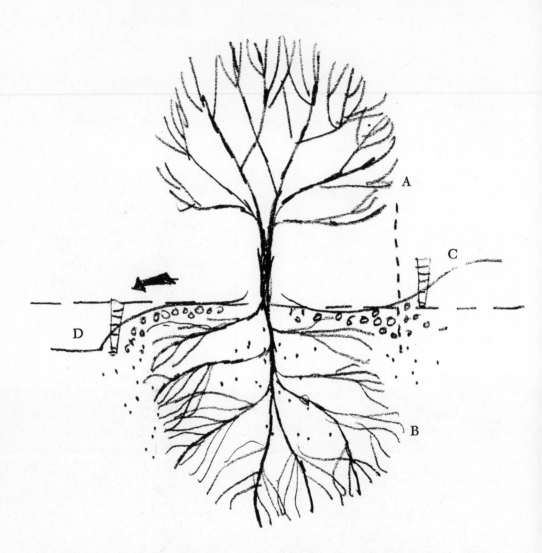

When the level must change on either side of a tree—up (C) or down (D)—
the best procedure is to build a wall outside the drip line AB.

4. Maximum thickness of the layers of the fill to be completed
5. Method of compaction
6. Density requirements of the completed fill, depending upon its location
7. Tests required during the process of filling.

Compaction should be done under the supervision of a licensed engineer.
It usually involves the placement of fill in thin layers, with the right moisture

content (neither too wet nor too dry), and with heavy equipment such as a sheep's-foot roller applied to them the proper length of time. Compaction will remove the main hazard produced by grading: the movement of loose filled ground when it gets wet. Cuts may, of course, create hazards if they remove support from material above and bring it down on the cutter's head.

Deviations from the standards may be permitted if supported by a licensed civil engineer in writing, or flatter cut or fill slopes may be required if necessary to stability and safety.

COMPLICATIONS IN GRADING.   Terracing or grading is most easily and cheaply done when nothing at all exists on the lot. This is another argument in favor of the over-all general plan before start of any actual work. If all the levels in garden and house are thought through completely beforehand, many difficult, expensive, and at times impossible problems will be avoided. It is much easier to dig the swimming pool in the back yard *before* the house is built.

Changing the natural grade (slope or ground surface) by filling creates problems for the footings and foundations of buildings or other structures. Unless the fill is compacted, these footings will have to be extended down through it to undistributed natural ground.

Changing existing grades also creates a problem through its disturbance of the natural relations between topsoil, subsoil, and bedrock. This can be avoided by a simple and reasonable process of stripping all existing topsoil from areas which are to be graded or built over or paved, stockpiling it, controlling the rough grades to allow for desirable depths of topsoil or paving on the finished site, and replacing the topsoil where it is needed for planting. It takes several hundred years to build a layer of good natural topsoil. This should not be wasted or buried to save a few dollars on grading costs. These dollars saved will then have to be spent to haul in new topsoil from elsewhere, if we expect healthy vegetation in the garden.

Changes in existing slopes disturb and alter existing surface, and sometimes subsurface (underground), drainage relations. The results of this disturbance, if not carefully planned beforehand, are apt to be complex, uncomfortable (if not disastrous), difficult to trace, and expensive to put under control. On a large scale, this situation involves major engineering for flood control, but every little garden has a miniature of this engineering problem within its own boundaries. Often it takes only a slight disturbance of existing drainage patterns to prove this.

There is, finally, the complication in grading when existing trees or other elements are already on the site. When such elements are to be preserved, they determine the level of terracing or grading in their immediate vicinity.

Structures determine it exactly, trees within a few inches or feet. The amount of cutting or filling that can be done around a tree is always a specific problem that must be solved on the job, considering the kind of tree, its size and form, the kind of soil and character of subsoil drainage, the wetness or dryness of the local climate, and so forth. The old problem of when to save and when to cut the tree is also always specific, always requiring careful judgment and thorough consideration, on the job, of all the horticultural, functional, and esthetic aspects before action is taken.

Drainage

Drainage is the great bugaboo of the new home owner, often forgotten and seldom completely solved before the first winter rain or spring thaw forces action. On sloping land each neighbor receives water from those above him, and deposits it on those below. Therefore a pattern of compulsory mutual responsibility is established. This is expressed in a pattern of legal relations as well as in physical relations. The act of excavating or filling, of destroying the natural vegetative cover, or of building impervious roof or paved surfaces increases the amount of surface runoff after rainfalls or snow thaw, and changes its direction and concentration. Therefore, unless it is controlled from top to bottom of your property, it can do serious damage to it or to the neighbors below.

SURFACE DRAINAGE. Control of surface water means keeping it moving, but not too fast unless in an impervious channel or pipe. The speed of movement of water is determined by the steepness of the slope and the smoothness of the surface over which it moves. Water will make a bog if moving too slowly, but it will make gullies if moving too fast. It is usually better to keep water moving on the surface of the ground than beneath it in pipes, because of the danger of these pipes' getting stopped up at just the wrong time. However, we are often forced to turn to catch basins and tile lines in order to preserve approximately level terrace areas. It is usually well to slow down runoff and let the soil absorb as much as possible, especially in areas of less than 25 in. of rainfall per year.

SUBSURFACE DRAINAGE. Subsurface drainage is the rate of movement of water below the surface of the ground. This is primarily a vertical movement, although at times the direction may be changed by strata of impervious material. In sand subsurface drainage is very fast; in clay it is very slow; in most soils, in between. This factor has a great deal to do with the kinds of plants which can be used in a specific garden, and with their health, once planted. While there are plants which will grow well in both extremes of fast and slow drainage, most garden plants require a medium or optimum condition. You can check this drainage in your garden very easily by digging a hole and filling it with water. If it disappears immediately or very soon, the drainage is probably too fast. If it takes two or three days to disappear, the drainage is too slow.

Fast drainage usually occurs in sandy or gravelly soils. It can be slowed down by incorporating large amounts of organic matter with the top two or three feet of soil. Organic matter may be peat moss, manure, leaf mould, compost, or the like. One may even put special plants in large pits lined with straw or moss and wire netting, or even wood, to hold back the water.

Slow drainage can sometimes be helped mechanically, by the incorporation of quantities of sand or other coarse material in impervious soils. It can sometimes be helped chemically, by the application of gypsum or soil sulfur, or some of the special trademarked preparations. Strangely enough, the incorporation of large quantities of organic matter is as helpful to these heavy soils, by opening them up, as it is to light soils by binding them together. On heavy ground which has not yet been planted, the application of raw green manure is very beneficial, if it can be left thirty days or more before planting. The deepest possible cultivation at the time of such additions is very important. In extreme soils we may have to resort to mechanical drainage with a horizontal underground grid of blind gravel drains or agricultural tile. Sometimes vertical holes drilled through heavy soils will reach lower strata of sand or gravel which will provide adequate drainage. Even without such strata, holes can be drilled under trees and shrubs and filled with gravel, to assist the plant in getting a start. On sloping ground tree and shrub pits can be drained out at the surface below with pipe or gravel.

All of these mechanical correctives have a limited relevance unless they are so complete as to change the entire volume of soil in which the plants will grow. Trees, especially, will sooner or later outgrow the area of mechanical correction. They may then begin to fail, which will be a great disappointment. Local practice and experience are usually the best guides when such problems seem too complex.

Soil Conditioning

Soil conditioning is concerned with the texture, the chemical and organic content, and the drainage properties of the particular soil on the particular site. It is concerned with these as they will affect the growth of

the plants intended for the garden. Plants may be selected which will grow in particular soils, or soils may be corrected to provide the right conditions for particular plants. Generally we do both of these things, within the limits of reasonable possibility. (See the discussion under "Plants and Planting.")

In general, most ornamental plants require a medium condition of soil, not too sandy, rocky or clayey; that is, not too many large or small particles, nor much that hasn't been exposed to action by weather, other plants, animals, and man. Most plants require in their soils a good content of organic matter, derived directly or indirectly from other plants. This includes the active population of microorganisms (soil bacteria and fungi) which is essential to good relations between plant roots and the soil. Most plants require adequate drainage; that is, water must move through the soil and beyond the root area within at most a few days. This is essential to the air circulation which most roots require in the upper layers of soil.

Experts will tell you that the above remarks are oversimplified. They will tell you of the various types of soils developed by the differing climate and vegetation patterns in these United States. An excellent short discussion is given by Charles Kellogg in CLIMATE AND MAN. He covers soil formation, the relationship between climatic factors and soil, the principal soil types and their characteristics, the factors involved in soil fertility and productivity, soil exhaustion and renewal, and erosion. These are discussed from the point of view of the farmer, and of the complexity of soil problems.

Soil management in the private garden can be as scientific as in agriculture, but limitations of space, time, and energy are apt to force it to be simpler, more intuitive, or more generalized. Typical patterns for handling typical soils develop within localities and regions. Gardeners learn from each other through clubs, schools, trade literature, and periodicals. In ordinary garden practice we try to provide soil conditions adequate for our plants by:

1. *Adding Material:* Adding and incorporating material lacking in the soil (such as chemical nutrients, earthworms, and organic matter).

2. *Texture Improvement:* Improving the texture, by adding sand to clay, deflocculating adobe with gypsum or soil sulfur, or incorporating organic matter with either extreme.

3. *Drainage Control:* Controlling the surface drainage, and adjusting the subsurface drainage if it is too fast or slow.

4. *Replacement:* As a last resort, if the existing soil is too bad, removing it and replacing it with good soil from elsewhere, if available.

5. *Composting:* The basic soil conditioner for all extremes except the boggy is organic matter, containing both humus and microorganisms. There are many sources of this, some common and some trademarked and copyrighted. However, the best and most basic source is that civilized process

William Aplin

Special drain by JACK
LITTLEFIELD, LAND-
SCAPE CONTRACTOR

known as composting. This involves returning to the soil that which came from it—grass cuttings, hedge and flower trimmings, fallen leaves, vegetable refuse, chopped brush—by rotting it down in a pile or pit with soil or manure in layers. There are many variations and details of this technique which can be found in the literature of organic gardening. Basically, however, it is in common-sense opposition to the wasteful and lazy process of burning or hauling away such material. This is soon followed by the hauling in of new and more expensive prepared organic material, such as manure, leaf mould, processed sludge, and so on. If your garden space is not big enough for a compost pit or pile, the possibility of a neighborhood or community compost plant should be explored.

6. *Absorbing Runoff:* Finally, in the dry half of the country (and in many dry spots in the wet half), the supply of underground water can be maintained and improved by slowing down and catching runoff precipitation water in spots where it can be absorbed by the ground to maximum capacity. This is better than the quick and apparently practical methods for getting rid of the water as rapidly as possible, in impervious pipes or channels.

These remarks should be considered merely an outline of the principal factors involved in soil conditioning. Detailed know-how on materials and techniques should be sought from your local soil experts, garden consultants, and materials distributors.

Utilities

The primary utilities in the garden are water lines, often electrical conduit, sometimes gas or sewer lines if separate play rooms, dressing rooms, or guest rooms are projected. Throughout the arid West, and in many occasionally dry spots in the humid East, the water lines are the life lines of the planted portions of the garden. Therefore the irrigation system—whether it is only hose bibs 50 ft. apart or a complete automatic sprinkler system— must be planned completely as a sympathetic part of the planting plan. At least the main lines should go in as soon as all the rough grading is done, before any other work. This applies also to the other utilities, particularly to hard waterproof conduit for garden lighting. This is a garden amenity which is becoming so popular as to be seldom forgotten, though often deferred for reasons of economy.

Paul J. Peart

6. Surfacing

Surfacing creates the floor of your garden living space. Once the problems of drainage and soil-conditioning have been worked out, the utility lines established, and the finished grades (slopes and levels) determined, then the treatment of all this exposed and disturbed ground surface must be decided.

In the average garden or yard space this treatment cannot be left to nature, because a natural cover of rough grass, weeds, or dead leaves is seldom suitable for the use such space is given. Surfacing materials must be employed which will provide adequately for the wear-and-tear of traffic planned for the area, and also control dust, dirt, mud, heat, glare, weeds, and surface drainage.

This means that the use must be analyzed and planned before surfacing materials are chosen. Such planning will often produce patterns composed of four basic types of surfacing: paving for heavy traffic, lawn for less-used areas, ground cover for areas in which no one will walk, cultivated beds for flowers or fruiting plants.

Yet these patterns of surfacing are more than functional; they are highly important in the composition of the garden picture. In many gardens they are the most interesting elements, and may be as carefully designed as expensive rugs. This tendency becomes questionable when patterns of low planting and paving distract attention from good views, or reduce the three-dimensional spaciousness of the garden. It is especially unfortunate for surface patterns to take precedence over enclosure and shelter elements, for these are much more important in the total garden picture, and only after they have been determined can a decision be made as to how elaborate or simple the ground pattern should be.

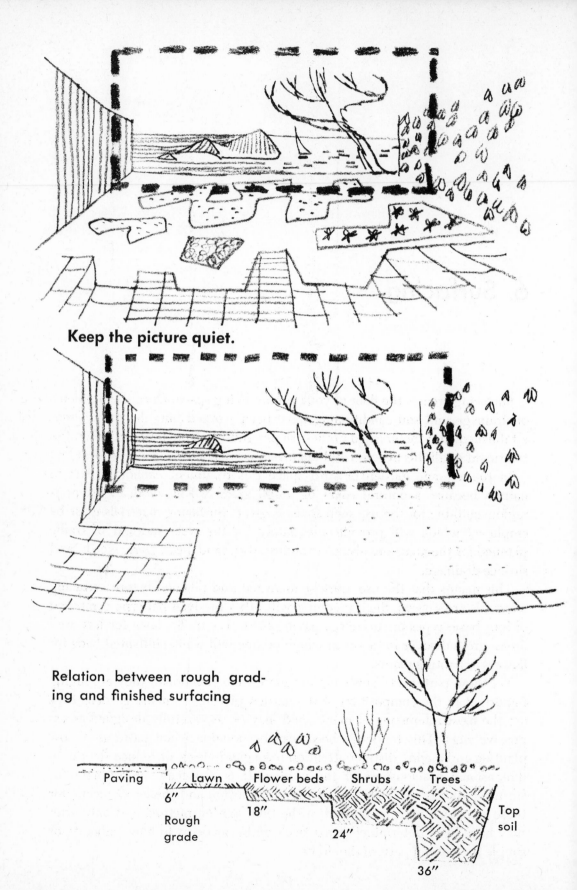

Keep the picture quiet.

Relation between rough grading and finished surfacing

Paving Lawn Flower beds Shrubs Trees

6″

Rough
grade

18″

24″

36″

Top
soil

The simplest forms and patterns—primarily rectangular—are generally the best choice. More complex forms should be used only when there is an obvious reason for using them, and only by confident planners. They should always be balanced and complete within themselves; one angle or one curve in a rectangular plan seldom has meaning and is usually discordant.

Decisions on surfacing are also related to decisions on foundation elements, for rough grading must allow for either thickness of paving or depth of topsoil. Grass and ground cover need 6 to 12 in. of topsoil, cultivated beds 18 to 24 in., and shrubs and trees 2 to 4 ft. The top surface of paving, or of soil prepared for planting, is called "finished grade."

Hard Paving

The most costly surfacing technique is hard paving, but it also requires the least maintenance, stands the most wear and tear (if properly installed), and gives the most permanent and precise control of surface and drainage. However it does absorb heat and create glare, a factor often forgotten in modern plans calling for large areas of paving.

Hard paving can be done with poured concrete or with unit materials, which include: brick, stone, tile, precast concrete blocks, stabilized adobe, wood blocks, and decking. The masonry units are usually laid in mortar on a rough slab of poured concrete. If they are not too thin, they may also be laid dry, in sand or sandy soil, with open or tight joints. This dry laying is popular with the amateur week-end worker because it can be stopped at any time without special precautions. It also feels softer and looks more rustic than paving done with mortar.

When choosing paving materials, remember that the forms and properties of the units should be related to the areas where they are to be used. Brick, tile, precast concrete, adobe, and milled wood are all rectangular or hexagonal units, and should be used in rectangular or hexagonal patterns. It is true that some of them, such as brick, can be cut, but the cutting is laborious, and the forcing of neat rectangular units into fussy irregular shapes is seldom worth the effort. Irregular areas should be paved with poured concrete, or with irregular units such as rough flagstone or redwood log sections. Flagstone and log sections are of such interest in themselves that they need not be confined within any specially shaped or outlined area. Wood decking (which must of course be protected from dampness and decay) is most commonly used to extend floor or paving where the ground slopes away too rapidly or is too soft to pave, but because of its lightness, springiness and flexibility it is sometimes chosen for level ground.

Poured concrete may be preferred for irregular areas because it is more flexible than flagstone or redwood. Thanks to modern methods of coloring and surfacing, concrete no longer needs to be dead, dull, and gray. Color may be dusted over the wet mix or applied as an acid stain after the concrete is cured; the first method produces a more even color and offers as wide a choice of colors as paint.

Use of special aggregates is another way to add interest to a concrete surface. These include selected pebbles and crushed brick, tile, or rock in various colors. They can be mixed in the top inch of concrete, or sprinkled over the surface after pouring and troweled in. Proportions must be determined by experiment.

After the concrete is partially set, it is brushed with running water to wash away the top ⅛-in. of cement and expose the special aggregate. The final refinement of this process is terrazzo ground smooth and polished—another surface which may be useful in the intimate garden. Mosaic paving, done by a specialist, is another refinement of this technique.

Climate must always be considered in the choice of paving materials. Extremes of heat, cold, moisture, or alternate wetting and drying place great strain on materals, as anyone knows who has seen the effects of heavy freezing and spring thaws on paved roads. Local conditions should be studied to see whether certain materials require special techniques, or should be eliminated altogether.

Soft Surfacing

The principal soft-surfacing methods include:

Stabilizing the soil with various lime or cement techniques, depending on soil texture and local atmospheric humidity

Use of fine decomposed rock, water-bound macadam, or crushed rock, wet and rolled for stability

Spreading a thin layer of sand, gravel, or crushed materials like tanbark or shavings.

Harder than these materials, but more flexible than the hard materials, are the various oil- or asphalt-bound surfaces: asphaltic concrete, bitumuls, and macadam. These are clean and flexible to use, but there are certain prejudices against them because of their association with paved streets, which monopolize such a large part of the outdoor area in our towns and cities.

LAWN. In common usage, "lawn" and "grass" are nearly synonymous. It is true that grasses are the most common materials used for lawns, but there

Soft

Childress-Halberstadt

Hard

Ernest Braun

Halberstadt

The lawn

are other lawn materials which may be chosen for reasons of use, maintenance, or appearance. In our definition, lawn is any planted ground cover
which will take a great deal of traffic—walking, sitting, or lying down.

Lawns may, of course, be developed primarily for appearance, and as
such may still perform the function of reducing glare, dust, and noise. However, even such areas as the front yard may be developed for use, as discussed in other parts of this book. Normally, a sign that says "keep off the
grass" is a sign of bad design or bad management or both. If normal use will
wear out a lawn, then the area should be paved, and trees or shrubs introduced to provide greenery. If paving is not necessary, adequate maintenance
for normal wear should be provided.

Maintenance, as we have said, is a factor in the choice of materials. The
tapis vert (the ornamental equivalent of the putting or bowling green) is
usually held up to us as ideal, but for the homeowner who is neither striving
for horticultural perfection nor prepared to provide meticulous weeding,
watering, fertilizing, mowing, and edging, such exact green carpets may
not offer the best solution. Various mixes of bluegrass and bentgrass and
fine fescues, plus nurse crops and clover and daisies, are generally more
interesting and more flexible, and adapt themselves more easily to varying
conditions of soil, sun, and shade. On steep banks, narrow strips, or extended
tortuous bays which are useless for sitting and irrelevant to pattern, the use
of any grass which requires mowing is apt to be a waste of both material
and labor. However, in large areas which justify the use of the power
mower, grass is the most pleasant and most easily maintained ground control.

After mowing, the greatest annoyance in lawn maintenance is edging.
Design which encloses the lawn with paving will greatly reduce this problem. Where the lawn is bordered by shrubs or uncut ground cover, a transi-
tional zone of tight mat-forming material, such as dichondra or lippia, may
remove the need for hand-trimming the grass next to the taller planting.
Another attempt to deal with mowing and edging problems has been made
in the South, where experiments have been made with grass substitutes such
as dichondra, lippia, chamomile, and creeping thyme.

GROUND COVER.   For areas which are not suitable or needed for living
purposes, ground cover planting can be used. Basically any plant whose
horizontal dimension tends to exceed its vertical is potential ground cover
material, if used in the right place. All sorts of plant forms are included: mat-
formers, trailers (vines without support), sprawling shrubby vines, and
spreading shrubs.

In practice, the ground covers most used are plants which are most easily
handled in quantity and most easily propagated, because large quantities
of the material are usually required. These include:

Ground covers

1. Seed (cover crops)
2. Material which can be handled as unrooted cuttings
3. Material which can be handled in small size in quantity, either from the field or in flat boxes (ivy, ajuga, wild strawberry).

It must be remembered, however, that a shrub which will eventually spread to cover 8 ft. will do the work of 50 small plants set 1 ft. apart. If time allows, shrubs may be the best choice, but cost and appearance must also be considered.

Uses for Ground Cover. Wherever paving, lawn, or cultivated beds are not desirable, ground cover may be introduced. Sometimes a better solution can be produced by extending ground cover to eliminate some or all of these other surfacings. Fill and soft-cut banks, and any slope greater than 15:100 vertical to horizontal, or 15 per cent, are best planted with such covers. They are more interesting in color and texture, and flourish with less care than grasses under similar circumstances, particularly on dry, sterile, or rocky slopes. Around buildings, ground covers are superior to paving or structural controls for reducing heat, dust, noise, and glare.

Ground Cover as Design. Beyond such practical considerations, ground cover plants constitute a design element of considerable importance. The larger kinds of shrubs which grow up to or above eye level become also enclosure elements, obstructing or baffling vision as well as movement. Below eye level there is a considerable range in heights, as from 3 in. up to 4 ft., within which very rich and interesting relations in form, color, and texture are possible. Here ground-cover planting begins to take on some of the functions of the herbaceous border. The distinction between the two is simply that ground-cover planting is relatively permanent; herbaceous border planting relatively impermanent. There are many kinds of perennials, bulbs, tubers, succulents, cacti, and even annuals which are so durable or persistent that they can be classed as ground-cover plants. Herbaceous and ground-cover planting can of course work together, if we determine clearly how much and how often we want to cultivate the ground. Where, to conserve water or labor, grass is eliminated, paving, ground cover, and trees can be expanded and related in new proportions and patterns of shade, greenery, color, and spacious surface.

Ground Cover Problems. Two problems primarily limit the use of ground-cover planting. The first is the cost or labor of installing all but the seeded kinds. This has to be balanced off against the long-term maintenance load. The second is weeds. Many a ground-cover planter's spirit has been broken by the struggle to keep out weeds the first year or two, until the ground has been covered. Even after that, if the supply of water and nutrients proves inadequate, the planting may fail to resist the invasion of undesirable weeds or grasses. Basically the ground cover planter should: first, kill off all weeds latent in the soil by persistent watering and cultivation, or the careful use of chemical weed killers, before planting; second, remove invading weeds regularly until the planting has covered the ground; third, keep the planting so healthy, with water and fertilizer, that it can smother any further invaders.

Trees as Ground Cover. One specific variant of the ground cover idea is the planting of trees so close together that their tops mingle and form a canopy above ground. These then perform the functions of ground cover—protecting the ground from erosion, reducing heat, dust, noise, and glare—and yet leave the ground surface clear for living activities. Some of it may be planted with shade plants, if their cultivation is not harmful to the trees; some may be surfaced with dry material; some may remain as bare packed ground. Careful selection of kinds of trees for density and season of foliage and dormancy will give very accurate control of sun and shade.

CULTIVATED AREAS. Cultivated beds, in which regularly or period-ically the existing plants are removed, the soil turned over and replenished, and new plants put in, are the garden proper. These are areas for flowers, vegetables, or seasonal crops. Here the horticultural routine reigns supreme, as described in endless garden manuals. You must decide for yourself whether this routine is fun or a chore. If you like gardening, the rewards are great—but you can have a perfectly pleasant and livable garden without these specialized activities. Here we encounter the distinction between gardens for gardeners and for nongardeners, which we discuss under planting maintenance. You must of course bear in mind that almost all planting will benefit from occasional surface cultivation, which aerates the soil and aids the penetration of water and nutrients. This is a much less arduous activity than true gardening.

Changes in Level

Changes in level, and connections between levels, introduce special surfacing problems in the garden. We have mentioned the use of lawn on slopes flatter than 15:100, and of ground cover planting on steeper slopes. The need for structural retaining elements, which are apt to be costly or laborious to build, appears in general where areas are so limited that space cannot be allowed for planted banks at the normal angle of repose between levels, or where soil and moisture conditions make that angle quite unpre-dictable. At times retaining elements may also be introduced for more esthetic reasons, as to expand a building into its site by the extension of the foundations beyond the walls. Often a low wall is necessary along the toe of a disturbed slope above a garden, to control the material which falls from it, and to establish a clean boundary between the refined garden and the rougher slope treatment.

Since these retaining elements are directly in contact with the soil, they must be of rock, masonry, or decay-resistant wood. Such structural assistance may take various forms, which merge one into another.

SLIGHT SLOPES.   If we begin by incorporating rock with the face of a bank in a more or less natural (irregular) manner, the rock can be distributed with increasing regularity and evenness, up to a surfacing of pebbles sorted to size, or cobblestones, flagstones, or masonry units. This can be combined with planting to develop any sort of pattern on the raised plane of the bank surface on slopes no steeper than 2:1, horizontal to vertical.

INTERMEDIATE SLOPES.   For intermediate slopes (from 1:2 to 2:1) certain techniques developed in highway work may prove useful. These involve the use of wood grids laid on the slope and filled with topsoil, which is then covered with straw and with coarse wire mesh spiked down. Portions of this may be used alone: straw and wire mesh, or straw alone cultivated into the slope. On any of these treatments, ground cover is seeded or planted. The surfacing holds the soil until the planting takes hold and stabilizes it. Success cannot be guaranteed with any of these without careful analysis of on-the-spot conditions of slope, soil, moisture, climate, and planting.

STEEPER SLOPES.   As slopes requiring retention approach the perpendicular without exceeding 6 ft. in height, dry unit surfacing merges into dry walls and bulkheads.

Dry walls are defined as gravity retainers with open joints, which allow water pressure (the principal nemesis of retaining walls) to dissipate itself by continuous drainage. Gravity retainers hold their position by sheer weight alone. Typically they are constructed of rough stone or boulders, broken concrete, or other miscellaneous masonry elements.

Since it has earth joints, the dry wall is the happy and practical home for the collection of alpines, succulents, and similar small plants requiring sharp drainage.

Bulkheads of redwood or other decay-resistant woods are satisfactory in mild climatic regions; they become less reliable as extremes of temperature or moisture and dryness become greater. They hold their position through

Ernest Braun (2)

Changes in level

William Aplin

proper spacing and depth of posts, or through being tied back to heavy "dead men" buried behind them. For loose fills, open cribbing of precast concrete, railroad ties or heavy durable creosoted timbers, constructed before or with the fill, is both practical and handsome. This, too, can be planted.

MORE DIFFICULT SLOPES. As the problem of bank retention becomes more difficult, because of height, soft material, moisture, or intimacy, we must go to solid masonry retaining walls. These also have their progression: from stone, brick, or concrete block, laid up in mortar, with or without reinforcing, to that last word in engineered reliability, the poured concrete wall.

All of these must provide drainage release for water pressure. Below 3 ft. and without complicating conditions (such as earthquakes) walls may be of the gravity type; solid masonry which stays in place by its own weight. With greater height, a slope above the wall, or special conditions of soil and moisture, the reinforced vertical cantilever, on a broad footing which is held by fill behind the wall or resists overturning in front, is most reliable. It must, however, be designed by an engineer.

This technical progression is likewise a progression in responsibility. Dry construction is relatively simple and direct. It can be worked out practically on the job with good workmen, offers little resistance to water pressure, but is limited in the heights and loads it can carry. Wet (laid in mortar or poured) masonry walls can be developed to meet practically any height and load requirements (a dam is a retaining wall for water). But, as they increase in size, their demands for technical excellence in design and installation (hence cost) increase also. Problems of retention are an apt field for structural ingenuity. Where there is space horizontally, the simple gravity or reinforced wall which is serpentine or sawtooth in plan will carry greater loads than a straight wall.

Connections Between Levels

Connections between levels, a special field for ingenuity and common sense in design, may be by steps, ramps, or their combination: ramped steps. Their design is determined by the relations between vertical and horizontal distances on the job. It is best, in terms of design scale as well as physical comfort, to spread such connections horizontally as much as possible. There is, however, also some need for compressing such connections. Often it is well to have both, to be able to go down fast but come up slowly.

TREADS AND RISERS. In steps the relation of 6-in. riser to 12-in. tread (in general the minimum slope indoors) should be the maximum slope outdoors. Outdoor steps are better looking and more comfortable if lower and broader. The maintenance of proper relations between tread and riser dimensions is of crucial importance. If steps are uncomfortable or unpleasant, it is usually because this relation is wrong. In broadening from the 6:12 ratio, the generally correct proportions are: 5-in. riser, 15-in. tread; 4-in. riser, 18-in. tread; 3-in. riser, 24-in. tread.

Flatter than this are ramped steps, typically risers 3 to 6 ft. apart with some slope between. Maximums are 6-in. risers and 1-ft. rise in 6 between. The maximum slope for a simple ramp is 15:100.

Within these general relations, many obvious interpolations and variations are possible, but the general proportional progression in broadening must be followed to produce functional connections. Where combinations of steps and landings are used, it is best not to hit a landing with the same foot twice in succession. Steeper steps, even prefabricated iron spirals or wooden ship's ladders, may be used in special spots for quick connection or special experience, but only occasionally.

The materials for these inter-level connections are compounded of those for surfacing and those for retention. Thus we can have wood risers with grass, sand or gravel treads, wood risers and treads on the ground, massive steps of log sections or large blocks, and free-standing framed wooden steps. Likewise we can have masonry steps of solid blocks laid dry, smaller blocks, as brick, in mortar, and poured reinforced concrete.

Steps and paths generally have to be considered as more than mere circulation elements. Design in those terms alone invariably makes them too small and cramped, more obvious in the general landscape because they are obviously out of scale with it. Most extreme example is the stepping stone, that coy speckling of little pieces of stone or concrete across lawns, too small and improperly spaced for walking, calling attention to itself by its very self-conscious spottiness. This must not be confused with the legitimate and well-designed use of large pieces of stone or wood, or sections of concrete, distributed regularly or irregularly (but always at walkable distances) throughout grass or other softer areas.

Scale is the primary problem. By this we mean the relation between the dimensions of the various parts of the garden, the dimensions of the entire garden space, and the dimensions of the landscape seen outside the garden. Steps, paths, and scattered units of paving must all be carefully related to both the scale of human use and the general scale of the specific landscape. This sense of form develops with experience. It cannot be put into rules, but the scale will generally be better as the elements are made larger rather than smaller. Steps, as abstractions of natural contours, can play a major role in both the sculptural expression of ground forms and the integration of buildings and outdoor construction with the site. Fear of "monumentality" or "ostentation" will make it impossible to realize this potential.

Scale and Selection

How do you decide which of the types of surfacing (paving, lawn, ground cover, and cultivated beds), or how much of how many of them, to use in your garden? Here is the central problem, around which all the others revolve. It can only be solved by making a complete analysis of all the conditions and needs of your garden—that is, by making a plan. The analysis must consider many factors:

Costs: How much freedom does your budget allow?

Use: How much human activity will there be in the garden?

Inside Comfort: How will various surfacings affect problems of heat, light, moisture, noise, and dust inside the house?

Appearance: What will the surfacing pattern look like in relation to enclosure and shelter elements, both from the house and from various spots in the garden?

Maintenance: How much regular or occasional labor and materials will be required to keep the surface in good condition?

Hard paving is most expensive to install, least to maintain; it will give most use with little or no maintenance; it does create certain problems of house comfort, unless it is properly handled; it can look well, if well designed. Hard pavings must be designed in detail and finish very carefully.

Soft pavings are quite inexpensive but are not as durable or as usable; problems of house comfort are not quite as great, except for dust, which may be bad; in appearance they are generally unobtrusive, hence careful design is not quite so important, except in terms of area and shape.

Lawn is quite inexpensive to install, but the maintenance is high, as we know; it will survive a reasonable amount of use, is less useful in wet country than dry; it is good for house comfort, and generally pleasant in appearance.

Ground cover planting is somewhat more expensive to install, has high maintenance at first but this tapers off rapidly; it allows no use of the area; it is good for house comfort, and generally pleasant in appearance.

Cultivated beds are about as expensive as ground cover to install, and have continuous high maintenance; they provide high use in terms of horticultural activity; they do less for house climate comfort than other kinds of planting, and look well only if well designed and maintained.

7. Enclosure

Enclosure forms the sides of your garden room. It may consist of planting: shrubs and hedges; or of construction: fences and walls. This enclosure has several functions:

1. It controls who can see into your garden, and what you can see out from it
2. It controls the movements of people (including children) and animals, keeping them in or out
3. It can be planned to control some wind and noise, and low morning and afternoon sun.

Since the design of the garden enclosure is much more flexible than that of the house, it can be high and solid where you need privacy or a screen against an ugly view, or thin, low, or nonexistent where you want the garden to be open. If the enclosure is required only to control movement, a wire fence or some similar solution will serve the purpose without blocking a view.

But besides these more or less obvious functions, garden enclosure has a more special and subtle function: to define space in the third dimension, just as the walls of a house define the rooms. Vertical physical elements give the sense of size, form, scale, proportion, and intimacy or grandeur which distinguish one living space from another; without them a garden becomes flat and dull. But it would also be dull if the vertical elements were all of the same size and weight and arranged in the same manner. We enjoy the contrast of open space with complete enclosure. If all rooms indoors and out were the same size and shape, our world would be a prison, and we would all go mad. Some of our large-scale postwar tract housing approaches this scale, and all the dishwashers, clotheswashers, and electric mixers in the world cannot compensate for it.

Enclosure elements are more important to the eye than surfacing patterns, because they are directly in the line of sight, at eye level. Take a look at the accidental enclosure elements of an unplanned back yard and you will see a miscellany of fences, sheds, and shrubs—some supplied by the owner, some by the neighbors. Obviously the first and most important job in improving that backyard is to clean up, rationalize, and simplify those enclosure elements. This is comparable to recognizing walls—and relations between solid walls, glass, and doors—as the most important elements in a room.

In planning or improving the enclosure elements of his garden, the home planner would do well to analyze them somewhat as follows:

Size: How high should the elements be, and how thick?
Weight: Should they be solid, translucent, or transparent?
Material: Are structural materials more appropriate than planting?
Detail: Exactly what material is best, and how should it be put together?

All of these factors, of course, must be considered in connection with the functions of enclosure discussed at the opening of this chapter. Now let us take a closer look at these factors.

Size

Height is the most important question to be decided, since it affects all of the functions for which enclosure is intended: control of vision, movement, wind, noise, and sun. Unwelcome observers may be on the same level as the garden, or higher, or lower, and so may undesirable views. Enclosure heights must be calculated accordingly. A fence intended to control the movements of small children or dogs can be much lower than one intended to keep out intruders. Height also has a direct effect on the amount of wind, noise, and sun that can be controlled, since an enclosure can control these elements only if they strike below its top. In general, insofar as the quality of the space is concerned, larger areas require taller enclosures. Function and appearance may require other proportions, however, regardless of the size of the area. Many zoning ordinances do not permit fences higher than 6 ft., but within setback lines we should not be afraid of building them 8, 10, or 12 ft. high if necessary.

Thickness of enclosing elements, like height, is related to the size of the area, but thickness is subject to actual physical limitations. In large gardens,

Movement

John Robinson

Elements

Noise

Childress-Halberstadt

Harry H. Baskerville Jr.

Vision

some or all of the sides may consist of heavy structures, or of shrubs spreading to a width of 8 or 10 ft., but a small garden may be limited to a fence or wall not more than 6 or 8 in. thick. Where beds of impassable plants, horizontal treillage, or areas of water are used, thickness or width may be a factor in control of movement, and under some circumstances it may become the primary dimension of enclosure.

Weight is concerned with the density or solidity of the screen. Solid, continuous enclosures (construction or vegetation) are required for privacy and control of noise. In small yards—50 ft. or less—vegetation is not reliable for maintaining privacy unless maintenance is exceptionally good. Sun and wind may be controlled with solid barriers, or filtered through open structures or plants. Pierced barriers tend to absorb wind, while solid barriers deflect it without reducing its force. Bushy trees or large shrubs provide pierced barriers of natural growth. Frame structures covered with wire mesh, treillage, or a series of panels arranged in layers may also be used. Thickness is a primary requirement.

To control movement, enclosure need only be solid enough to prevent passage of human beings or animals. Wire mesh, treillage, or dense, stiff, or thorny plants will serve the purpose.

As for defining space, anything from solid walls to mere traceries or branches of treillage will establish a third dimension in the garden room, but a variation in density is interesting if possible. The translucent screen, which admits light but blocks both vision and movement, is a refinement which is as useful in the garden as in the house, and in the garden it may consist of foliage or close treillage, as well as of glass or plastic.

Materials

Enclosure may be accomplished with either structural or plant materials. Any *structural materials* can be used which will take the year-round weather in your locality without too much maintenance. *Wood and masonry* (in all their variations) are most common. These include split, rough-sawn and finished lumber; concrete block, brick, tile, stone, poured concrete; and stucco on wood frame or concrete block.

In addition, various *sheet materials* can be used, usually on a wood frame. These include plywood, hardboard, asbestos-cement, glass, plastics. Metal, in sheets, rods, or grids (chain-link fencing) is commonly used.

Odd or unexpected materials may prove surprisingly useful and handsome: pipe, canvas, glass block, bottles, celluloid on wire screen, and so on. Water is an enclosing element, because we cannot walk across it. Any slope, mound or ridge tends to become an enclosing element, to the extent that it restricts or obstructs movement or vision. Intermediate between structural and planted enclosure is the *open structure* (as a chain-link fence) supporting vines.

Plant materials for enclosure include any row, mass or grouping of plants tall enough to interfere with movement or vision.

Shrubs, small trees, conifers, tropical plants, cacti may be spaced close together or far apart to make solid enclosure or mere framing or tracery. For enclosing garden space at the sides, the best plants are those of more erect growth, usually taller than they are wide. Certain radial clump forms may be useful for either ground cover or enclosure. All of these plants possess various degrees of height, density, and evergreenness, and your selection will depend on what you want in the way of screening, privacy, and protection from intrusion by life, sun, or wind.

The range of choice in form, texture, and color is as broad as the available range of larger herbs, grasses, and shrubs; of trees; and of vines supported structurally. All the shrubbery border material—facer, filler, background—the hedge material, the smaller trees, the vines, the larger odds and ends that have been consigned to the wild garden, the cactus garden, the tropical or desert garden, or some other pigeonhole—take on new vitality, interest, and richness when considered as enclosure material. The less you need in the way of screening, privacy, and protection, the wider will be your choice of material. The solid plant screen gives you variations in color and texture of foliage. A less solid screen, used as space division within a general enclosure, can be more playful or imaginative, with variations in structural pattern, in relation of foliage to ground, and in fruit and flower color.

DETAIL. Enclosure elements are subject to endless variation in detail through varying relations of materials, design, ingenuity, common sense, and craftsmanship. In terms of their effect on garden space, structural details may be classified about as follows:

Low, blocking movement but not vision:
  Railings or open grids, of wood, metal, bamboo, tile, and the like
  Low solid walls and seats, of wood or masonry
  Pools and canals
Medium (4 ft. up) blocking movement and some vision:
  Rows of poles, with or without top rails
  Trellis or lattice frames, with or without glass or other fillers
  Louvered, split-wood, or other open-joint fences
  Pierced panel screens
  Masonry with openings

Aplin-Dudley Studios

Maynard L. Parker

1. Wood frame cellu-screen
2. Redwood posts; copper sculpture by Claire Falkenstein; precast concrete panels
3. Resawn lumber

$$\frac{1}{2}\Big|3$$

1. Split redwood fence; finished redwood seat
2. Wood deck and rail
3. Wood trellis, fountain, plywood
   wall

$$\frac{1}{3}\bigg|\frac{}{2}$$

Julius Shulman; courtesy Condé Nast

Morley Baer

Halberstadt

1

2

Morley Baer; courtesy House Beautiful

1. Wood grids and solid wood screens
2. Wood screen, glass windbreak, wood deck

1. Dowels on plywood
2. Redwood rail and seat
3. Redwood treillage

Julius Shulman

Stout

1. 4 x 4 redwood set diagonally; masonry wall beyond
2. Bamboo fence

Childress-Halberstadt

Maynard L. Parker

Medium (4 ft. up) blocking movement and some vision:
   Transparent or translucent sheets or blocks of glass or plastics
   Solid fences or walls to 5 ft. 6 in.
   Large ridges, mounds, or banks of earth
Tall (6 ft. or more), blocking movement and all vision:
   Solid wood
   Solid masonry
   Solid sheets or panels

The exact detailed design and construction of these elements is variable throughout the country. We can generalize in a few words points which seem important to us, and we can illustrate methods and details which have proved useful in our work. Beyond that, the reader will have to conduct his own explorations of local practices and materials.

Wood Construction

Lumber comes in standard framing dimensions: 2 by 2, 2 by 4, 4 by 4, 4 by 6, and so on. It also comes in standard sheathing and siding dimensions— 1 by 1 to 1 by 12, plain edge, shiplap, tongue-and-groove, and so on. There are many odd small fractional sizes in lathing, battens, mouldings, beads, edges, trim strips, dowels, poles, half- and quarter-rounds, and similar units, which are very useful in trellis work. The standard dimensions are rough-sawn or milled. Finished dimensions are somewhat smaller. Split palings and stakes, peeled saplings and poles approximate milled sizes.

Wood which is to come in contact with the ground must be decay-resistant—redwood or equal. Above the ground, any kind which will take the local weather can be used. Two-inch wood resists the effects of weathering best, although it may check badly if not properly finished. Thinner wood is more apt to warp, twist, cup, expand, contract, split, or buckle. It must therefore be used more carefully, and finished sooner with varnish, stain, or paint.

Proper attention must be paid to finishing any wood or metal construction with paint or stain. If you decide to let the wood weather, be sure you know just what weather will do to it.

WORKMANSHIP. In order to build a good fence or other structure one must be what is known as a good mechanic. It must be built to last, and to look as well in ten years or more as it does today. Garden structures, even more than houses, are subject to shoddy, jerry-building practices. Great care must therefore be taken to guarantee good, durable, handsome construction.

1

2

1. Wood grid, cellu-screen, brick seat
2. Patterned wall of pumice block, glass, and brick

The typical fence is supported by a series of vertical posts set solidly in the ground, with or without concrete, connected by horizontal stringers which support the vertical finish material. Fences may be built on concrete footings, but this is more expensive and makes vertical bracing more difficult.

Posts or footings must reach below the frost line in those major portions of the country where the ground freezes. Posts are generally placed 4 to 6 ft. apart, connected with two or three stringers (2-in. stringers for 4-ft. spacing, 4-in. for 6-ft). Sometimes the posts may be closer together and the stringers eliminated by the use of continuous horizontal finish material. This is especially useful for curved fences.

Every fence has two sides, and it is often a problem to decide which side to finish, unless we can afford to finish both sides. Much energy has been expended on fence details which are the same on both sides, in order to avoid this problem. Such details usually involve exposing the posts, and breaking the fence up into a series of panels, rather than a continuous wall. The latter is apt to be the more pleasing fence surface. The former requires more careful detailing and execution.

Posts must be truly vertical. Stringers must be truly horizonal. Finish material must be truly parallel, whether vertical, horizontal, or angular. This is the test of the well-built fence. Nothing is more disturbing than the fence or other structure in which the verticals, horizontals, or angles are slightly and irregularly off. This speaks of instability, insecurity, shoddy workmanship, and neglect. Fences which follow ground slopes at random have a careless and haphazard quality which destroys the sense of order and stability embodied in any good building.

GROUND SLOPE PROBLEMS.   Relating garden structures to variable ground slopes is a difficult and subtle problem. It requires extremely careful special study of the exact details of the problem. If the fence or wall will be seen primarily against or in close relation to the house, then it should be truly leveled, even if that demands certain structural complications. If it is seen primarily in relation to ground forms, or partially leveled terraces, then it can quite safely follow those slopes if they are under 4 or 5 per cent. It may even follow steeper slopes if it is separated from level structures, and if it is kept in simple straight-line forms, or perhaps simple curves. Otherwise the fence or wall should probably be either stepped or planted out; there is something very disquieting about a vertically serpentine structure. When it is seen in relation to both level buildings and slight ground slopes the problem becomes quite complex. Sometimes the difference may be split; sometimes stepped levels may be developed.

This emphasis on true verticals and horizontals is not a matter of abstract esthetics or artistic whimsy. Your physical security, as we have pointed out in Chapter 2, is maintained by aligning yourself with the pull of gravity. Horizontal surfaces are therefore most secure, and vertical and horizontal elements in the right combination feel most stable and well balanced.

Masonry Construction

Masonry, by contrast with the light, dry, and open character of frame construction, is solid, heavy, and durable throughout. It is a kind of synthetic stone, held together by cement, shaped to form according to plan and detail. This is true of the entire range of masonry structures, from the stone or brick wall held together by thin joints of mortar (sand and cement) to the poured concrete wall in which the cement, sand, and rock are the principal ingredients. Here again much must be learned from local craftsmen and materials dealers, and we can only generalize.

Basically masonry walls may be produced by either of two techniques: building up in layers with precut units and mortar; or pouring wet in wooden forms. Unit masonry may be of stone, broken or cut with varying degrees of roughness, accuracy, and polish; clay products such as brick and tile, which are cut to form when wet, then cured with high heat in a kiln; and precast concrete blocks, which have been formed wet in the factory. Clay products and concrete blocks are regular units, usually rectangular. Stone is quite irregular, even when sawn.

All of these units are laid up on a concrete footing which is poured in a trench dug into the ground. This footing must be adequate in width and depth to carry the weight of the wall and prevent it from turning over. In the north and east, where the soil freezes, it must go down below the frost line. Reinforcing steel is commonly used in masonry walls to bind them together horizontally and vertically, and to reduce the mass of material needed for stability by connecting vertical wall with horizontally spread footing in the engineered cantilever.

The sure touch of the good mechanic is even more essential to masonry wall construction. Rectangular clay and concrete units must be laid up in true horizontal and vertical courses, and the corners and ends must be plumb and sharp. Because of its weight, a masonry wall that has wavy horizontal joints, or is out of plumb vertically, is rather disquieting for us to look upon. One often encounters the problem of relating masonry walls to uneven or sloping ground. It must be solved even more carefully and skillfully than with wood. The objective is to produce a wall which feels horizontal and stable, even though it may possibly not be truly level. It is usually better and quieter to keep such walls in simple rectangular units, rather than to break them up with many steps, jogs, piers, or panels.

CLAY AND CONCRETE UNITS. Mass-produced clay and concrete building units (bricks, tiles, blocks) are regular and rectangular, in contrast to the irregularity of stone. There is an endless variety in the sizes and proportions of these precast units, and likewise in the various ingenious details for interlocking and bonding. Clay products have a common color range through tans and reds, expressing the passage of earth through fire. Concrete blocks, on the other hand, range from light to dark gray, the distinctive color of poured cement. Special blocks are now commonly produced in several colors (including some quite bilious pinks and greens) and in various forms and textures typically described by such trade names as Slumpstone and Flagcrete. The reader must choose with care among these. Some are very useful.

The possibilities of variation and imaginative treatment in the mixing, forming, and finishing of concrete are endless. The most refined forms, terrazzo and cast stone, almost complete the cycle back to mother rock again.

Both clay and concrete are also used in a wide variety of industrial and building units—various sorts of pipes, tiles, flues, and drainage boxes, circular, expanded-circular, or rectangular in section—which can be used imaginatively as well as practically in the garden. Consider, for instance, a wall of 12-in. lengths of 4-in. agricultural tile laid up across the wall as a trellis. There are also special forms of clay and concrete products, both ready-made and custom-made—such as ceramics and glazed tile—which are useful in enriching special parts of the garden.

ROCK MASONRY. Because of its variety of native characteristics and the many ways it can be handled, tooled, and processed, rock has a wide range of possible uses. This range may be suggested by the following, all relevant to garden enclosure:

Natural sculptural boulders or outcrops
Rough dry field-stone walls
Rough-cut stone with or without mortar
More and more careful hand cutting, fitting, and mortaring
Sawn stone
Polished granite or marble
Sculpture.

Rock, at whatever level of handling or processing, is always a highly individualized handicraft material. Each job is different, each job is new. Artistry

Morley Baer

Masonry has many patterns.

Paul J. Peart

Paul J. Peart

and common sense must be combined in varying proportions for best results. A feeling of stability and appropriateness may be achieved by placing
the rock as nearly as possible in the position it occupied in nature. This is
sometimes easy to determine, and sometimes practically impossible.

Sedimentary rocks, such as sandstone, shale, and limestone have been
laid down in such thin sheets as to show the strata lines when quarried, and
should always be laid with those strata marks horizontal. Indeed, even if the
strata may have been folded by geological pressures in some more or less
upright position, we should "induce nature to improve herself" by also laying
them horizontally.

Igneous and metamorphic rocks, on the other hand, which may have
formed in any sort of odd-shaped mass without special direction in the veining or crystalline structure, derive their stability from the shape of the block
of stone. Here again, horizontality is the primary principle. Most of the
blocks or pieces of stone should be longer than they are high, and the long
dimension should be placed horizontally. While one can find many attractive
exceptions to this rule, in various block, crazy-quilt, and boulder patterns, it
is nevertheless the simplest and most direct way to bring out that quality of
stability which is primary in rock and stone. This applies equally to the poor
man's stone wall, that of broken concrete.

ROCK AS SCULPTURE.   The remarks above apply particularly to stone
construction. That is, individual stone shapes merge into some larger, simpler, dominant form (a wall), within which the stone makes a three-dimensional pattern. Partial enclosure may also be achieved, where the occasion
warrants, by the alternative use of specific rocks—natural existing boulders
or outcrops, or collected water- or ice-formed boulders, concretions, and
igneous fragments of plastic or fantastic form—as sculptural specimens in
extended groups.

For such arrangements we find our best prototypes in the Orient. The
refinement, sensitivity, and maturity of concept exhibited in Chinese and
Japanese rock work has seldom been equaled in other garden cultures. Their
use is not naturalistic, in our sense of the word. They use rocks as sculptural
forms or groups; their aim is the intensification and expression of nature, not
her imitation.

Although sculpture normally means the carving of rock to produce designed forms, many natural rocks already have forms of sculptural interest.
Many sculptors try consciously to base their forms as much on the natural
form of the rock as on a selected subject or idea. This sculptural approach to
rock is useful in a variety of situations: taking advantage of existing natural
boulders or outcrops; rearranging or expanding them; creating new arrange-

Sculpture by Pegot Waring; photo by Lou Jacobs Jr.

Al Greene & Associates

Sculpture from rock

1. Enclosure by plants
2. Earth mound separation

ments with imported rocks or boulders; combining such sculptural rock forms with stone construction of any of the types enumerated. To be effective as enclosure elements such rocks need only to be large enough to obstruct movement or vision. In desert or mountain areas houses may be surrounded by fields of almost impassable rocks and boulders.

Planted Enclosure

The detail of planted enclosure is concerned with the selection and combination of various kinds of plants. This problem is considered in some detail in Chapter 10, on plants, but for enclosure purposes we are specifically concerned with a more organized or architectural pattern, with larger quantities of fewer kinds.

This is in contrast to the old-fashioned mixed shrubbery border, including a few each of many kinds. We make no hard and fast rules, and feel that all sorts of patterns and combinations of plants must be explored. However, the usual mixed border takes up too much space and tends to be fussy, spotty, restless, and shapeless.

Arrangement. In architectural enclosure patterns plants may be spaced regularly or irregularly in straight or curved lines or staggered rows—in order to develop their natural form and growth habits without too much restriction. Plants may be allowed to grow naturally, though planted in geometric patterns, just as they may be prevented from growing naturally, though planted in irregular "naturalistic" patterns. In fact, in average small gardens, more regular placement of greater numbers of certain kinds will display their qualities much more effectively than a scattered treatment. Arrangement according to a planned enclosure pattern makes it possible for people to come closer to all the plants in the garden, and therefore to experience them better.

Plant Selection. This kind of pattern does not necessarily mean fewer kinds of plants in the garden, although it can very well. We tend to use different kinds for different sections of enclosure, as for instance gray on the south wall, dark green on the north wall, yellow-green east and west. This type of enclosure pattern also makes possible the use of many specimens, in ones, twos, or threes, carefully placed in relation to the larger enclosure groups. Much variety is also possible with smaller herbaceous plants within such an organized framework.

Form Possibilities. Basically we feel that your garden experience will be improved if you get over the old fear of geometric plans as being unnatural, artificial, or rigid. The old-fashioned "formal garden" was apt to be all of these, but a geometric plan can be informal, irregular, and quite natural in feeling. This does not mean that you have to throw out naturally scattered groupings or freely curved or massed arrangements. We think gardens become richer and more beautiful when they use all these different form possibilities, and when they are not afraid to combine them in unorthodox patterns without regard to old-style formality, informality, or naturalness.

EARTH AS ENCLOSURE. The detail of earth forms is given in Chapter 3, on foundations. The form of mounds or ridges which may be useful for enclosure is governed by the angle of repose. The built-up slope should probably not be steeper than 2:1 (horizontal to vertical). This means that a ridge 4 ft. high on flat ground has to be at least 16 ft. wide.

Such forms are too space-consuming for use in the average garden. However, cut slopes can be as steep as 1:1, or even steeper, with structural assistance. Very often owners of lots of some slope, on which grading is necessary, can with ingenuity take advantage of this necessity to utilize the ground forms as part of the enclosure.

WATER AS ENCLOSURE. The detail of water forms as bounding or enclosing elements is primarily concerned with their size and form. They must be wide enough to keep one from stepping or jumping across, and long enough to function as part of the enclosure pattern. Ornamental pools in the centers of gardens and swimming pools close to houses both create obstacles to movement in unfortunate positions. They tend to make the garden feel smaller, less spacious, and more cluttered. Water recognized and used as an enclosing element will, on the other hand, increase the apparent size and space of the garden.

Containers for water in the garden are formed in various ways. In humid regions, where dense ground never dries out, they may be dug or hollowed out of the ground, or the planner may take advantage of existing depressions. Lower humidity or more porous soil may require that these be lined with some more or less impervious material: clay, building paper, asphalt, concrete. This need not show, and such pools or channels are treated as simple natural patterns of water.

Structural containers, designed to show above water or ground, may be of unit masonry or of poured concrete. The former must be waterproofed inside below the water line, and its design in general follows that of unit masonry enclosures and paving. The latter are monolithic sculptural forms which can take any shape, within the limits of the garden plan and the techniques of forming.

Water as enclosure

Julius Shulman; courtesy Condé Nast

In all of these, the source or means for getting water into the basin, and the method of preventing overflow, and of draining when necessary, must be designed with the container.

Decisions on Enclosure

How do you decide how much enclosure you need, whether it should be structural, planted, or mixed, and how it should be detailed? This is first of all a functional and practical question. You must analyze your property and its surroundings, in order to determine whether the views out from the garden are desirable. This determines whether they are to be screened from your view. You must also determine who can look in at you from outside, and whether you want to screen them out for privacy.

Typically elevated hillside lots, for example, have views and no privacy problem on the view side, hence no need of enclosure except to guarantee security from falling, or to guide the view up or out rather than down.

Typical flat lots, on the other hand, usually have no view out, and require complete screening enclosure for the sake of privacy. This is sometimes complicated by a fear of hurting the neighbors' feelings. But good neighbors should respect one another's privacy in the garden as much as in the living room or bedroom. The 5-ft. fence is high enough to hurt feelings, but usually not high enough to guarantee privacy. A higher fence is generally the better course, with channels for social contact established through front or back doors and gates.

More complicated problems of enclosure come when there is a good view on a side where there is also a privacy problem. These require careful study and ingenious solutions. The intensity of these screening problems increases as lots get smaller. Privacy is much easier to maintain on a half acre than on an eighth acre.

Screen enclosures will also control the movement of adults, children, and animals, as well as some sun, wind, and noise. Note again the discussion of enclosure functions at the beginning of this chapter, not forgetting the importance of three-dimensional effect. All of these must influence your decisions.

Codes. The zoning and building ordinances, governing setbacks and height limits in your locality, are important elements of your enclosure problem. Often these will make it more difficult to achieve the kind of enclosure you may need. A 6-ft. fence limitation on the property line may force you to plant shrubs to grow 10 or 12 ft. inside the fence. Or it may force you to move the fence inside the setback line in order to build it high enough.

Costs. Cost is, of course, the primary limiting factor, whether it is measured in dollars and cents or in cost of materials plus hours of your own labor. Compromise between ideal solutions and economics is almost always necessary. Too much compromise, however, will fail to solve the problem, and will render the whole project a waste of time. It is necessary to establish a budget and a plan of work, so that you know how much you can spend in a given period of time, what the first-priority elements in the garden are, and about what they will cost. This makes it possible to produce a complete solution over a period of months or years. It can be produced only if you have a fairly clear idea at the beginning of what the ultimate solution should be like.

Structure or Plants. Structural enclosures cost more than planted, unless the size of the plants used is such as to produce a complete screen immediately. Structural enclosure is more immediate and more permanent than planted, and requires less maintenance. It is subject to considerable design refinement, while planted enclosure can explore the possibilities of various plant textures and colors. Each of these serves different functions in relation to view, privacy, control of movement, wind, sun, noise, space formation, the existing building, and the existing topography.

Making the Plan. All of these questions of choice and selection of materials and details, of costs and functions, can be answered only within the framework of a complete plan for the garden. This plan must project the enclosure pattern as well as the ground cover pattern, so that the planner can think through the relations between the two. What kind of surfacing goes with what kind of enclosure? Does structural enclosure require structural surfacing? Should the same material be used on the floor as on the sides? And so on.

With your growing plan on the table, you can also think through the relations between the various functions of enclosure as they occur on your lot, and between the various kinds of materials and detailing that you might be able to use. In the experimental process of producing a plan on paper (costing little more than paper, pencil, and time, unless you hire some professional help) you avoid a much more tedious, agonizing, and expensive process of experimenting on the ground with real labor, real materials, and real dollars and cents.

Finally, the plan makes possible the design of your entire three-dimensional garden space, closely related to the house, in forms which are at least comfortable and restful, and at most beautiful and enriching to your life.

Garden designed by Douglas Honnold, Architect; photo by Donald J. Higgins

8. Shelter

We normally think of the garden as unroofed living space, open to the sky, by contrast with the complete enclosure of the house. This is the main reason for the emphasis on the quality of the side enclosure.

We have found, however, that there is no sharp break necessary between living inside the house and living outside. The two tend to overlap in the area immediately around the house. Here we are apt to find a need for an extension of the shelter function of the house roof. This will give partial or complete overhead protection to the primary outdoor living spaces, and also help to protect the house from climatic extremes. This is important in the control of such elemental forces as sun, rain, wind, snow, heat, glare, dust, noise, insects. Such supplementary shelter may be supplied by structures, vines on structures, or trees.

Shelter elements are at the same scale and have the same importance in the landscape as houses. If structures, they supplement the house, extending it into the garden, making it feel bigger, easing and strengthening the connection with the garden. Trees complement the house, balancing it with landscape elements of the same importance, framing it and settling it down on the land, and at neighborhood scale establishing a natural structural pattern which can integrate a collection of miscellaneous houses and unify the neighborhood landscape.

These shelter elements are of relatively greater architectural importance in the garden scheme than surfacing, which is primarily a ground pattern, or enclosure, which is generally at direct human scale, on the eye level rather than above it. Garden shelter may be provided with the original house, as porch, lanai, lath, or arbor extensions. Or it may be added when the garden

is designed, either joined directly to the house or as an independent structure; or it may consist of trees in the garden.

CODES AND PERMITS. The local building code or department
should be consulted before structural shelters are designed, if they are being
added after construction of the main dwelling. Often there are special rules
about when an additional structure is considered to be attached to the main
building, hence a part of it, and when not. Or there may be special ways of
determining whether or not a garden shelter comes under the provisions of
the code. Again, there may be special rules governing how far such elements
may project into front, side, or rear yards, or what proportion of those yards
such shelters may occupy.

For example, in some areas one may build an open frame arbor without
permit, setting the posts in the ground as for a fence. But if one should then
decide to place any sort of solid roofing over the top of this arbor it becomes
a roofed structure in the eyes of the building department. It then comes
under permit regulations, and must have its posts cut off and separated
from the ground by six inches of concrete. Immediately, of course, the structure will lose its rigidity and will have to have an entirely new bracing
system, and so on. Such problems are best avoided by foresight.

ESTHETICS OF SHELTERS. As with enclosure, shelter elements may
be used for direct rational functional control of the forces of climate, as enumerated, or they may be used in a freer and more esthetic way to provide a greater sense and definition of space overhead, greater connection
between house and garden, or softer transition from indoors to outdoors.
Usually these objectives are thought of and designed for together; each
helps the other. Here again the quality or feel of the garden space, as defined
overhead by structures or trees, is as important a functional or practical
question, because of its psychological impact upon you who live there, as
problems of sun, shade, or wind. The luxurious quality of a living area—no
matter how small or simple—which is half in the house and half in the
garden, having some qualities of each, has to be experienced to be understood.

Weather Control

Sun, heat, and glare are usually best controlled by filtering through
open patterns such as vegetation, lath, treillage, or netting, or through
translucent materials such as canvas, plastics, or glass. The former give

greater control, or allow greater reduction in quantity of sun, than most of the latter. The open pattern controls also allow greater circulation of air, which is usually an essential partner in the reduction of sun, heat, and glare.

Translucent materials are useful for light shade where summers are mild, and they do have the virtue of diffusing light evenly. The dappled light of the open pattern materials is sometimes hard on the eyes. The primary usefulness of the translucent materials is for shedding precipitation (rain and dew) without losing much light. They provide outdoor skylights and give warm shade, useful in cool, bright weather.

Rain, Snow, and Wind Control. Protection from rain and snow requires, of course, a solid and leakproof roof equal to that on the house. The solid shade of such a roof may be very welcome in hot weather, if provided by a structure of open sides which allow breezes to blow through. In cool regions where we want to escape from the wind or protect ourselves from it, both solid and open shelters will function with enclosure structures to increase the windbreak area and extend the quiet zone produced by it. The function of slanting shelters in diverting wind should not be overlooked.

SPECIAL CLIMATE PROBLEMS. Those sections of our country which have extreme variations between hot and cold, or wet and dry seasons, and hence require different kinds of shelter control at different months, pose special problems. In the East, hot-wet and cold-dry coincide; in the West, the reverse is true.

The simple formula of modern architecture, whereby a roof overhang is designed to a dimension which will keep out the summer sun and let in the winter sun, works only in regions where fall and spring are intermediate, and when the building faces true south. In southern regions, where the hottest weather may come in the fall, the problem is more complicated. Even in January and February there may be a week or more with temperatures above 85° every day, when shade is welcome.

In general, to solve this seasonal problem, we must do one of two things. We can design flexible shelters which will change with the seasons (deciduous trees or vines, if we have species which lose their leaves for approximately the right period of time), or frame structures with removable panels or sheets of material, such as canvas or shrimp netting. The frames may even be designed so as to swing out when needed, back when not, awning-style. As an alternative to flexible shelters we can design different garden areas for different seasons, if we have enough space.

No easy design solutions have been developed for the control of insects outdoors. However, large screened porches and enclosures have proved useful in many insect-ridden parts of the country. Special lights, smoke, or traps sometimes help. Insects are generally a community or regional problem requiring solution at that scale.

Shelter Details

The detailed design of shelter elements is as variable as the detailed design of houses and their planting arrangements. Structural shelter, since it is supplementary to the house, must partake in some manner of the character of the house in order to be harmonious with it. This does not mean that, if we happen to have a Georgian or Colonial house, we must make a frenzied search of the history books to find "appropriate" historical shelter forms to copy. It does mean that we must examine the house as a physical reality of specific materials and details.

These can be reflected in a specific and realistic way in the design of additional shelter elements, without being either "modern" or "traditional." Bearing in mind the great potential variability in the design of shelter elements stemming from current combinations of ingenuity, imagination, new materials, old forms, and new ways of looking at old problems, we can classify the possibilities into generalized types of structures.

Wood Structures. Structural shelters may be open, ranging from simple post-and-beam pergolas and arbors to the 50 per cent or more enclosure of lath houses and more elaborate treillage structures. These have many uses, including the extension of houses into their gardens, the connection of houses with other structures, the support of climbing roses and other flowering vines, the provision of filtered light for shade-loving plants and people. These are usually thought of as landscape structures: posts may be set in the ground for simple bracing, and there is a general tendency to make them somewhat too careless, rustic, or flimsy. Even with the simplest arbor there is no substitute for the use of members of adequate size for the loads and spans they must carry; for vertical posts set solidly in the ground or on footings; for horizontal or accurately sloped beams; for proper, strong, clean connections between members; and for proper finish with paint or stain.

Metal Structures. Traditionally the material for these open garden shelters has been wood, but metal, in all its many structural forms, has great possibilities for frames which are lighter and stronger than wood.

The techniques are primarily those of plumbing and welding, and these are generally available. The parts are usually best made up completely in the shop, which means that they must be more carefully designed beforehand. Metal is not so flexible as wood on the job. Iron and steel must be finished very carefully with paint or galvanizing to avoid rusting. Rustproof aluminum is now generally available.

Structural shelters of all weights

Frameworks of both wood and metal must be designed both for their own appearance, and for the lath, siding, plywood, or other panel material, or glass, plastic, wire screen, or fiber netting which may be added to them. Metal will cost more than wood, therefore is apt to be used only where extra strength or thinner members are worth extra cost. Open shelter structures are most flexible and open to imaginative development. These overhead patterns are both practical and esthetic in the garden.

Extending House Structure. Structural shelters may be closed either at top only, with solid roofs for complete shelter, or at some or all sides as well, to provide garden rooms, barbecue rooms, play and rumpus rooms, tea houses, screened porches, pavilions, casinos, cabanas, bathhouse-dressing rooms, work and storage spaces, and the like. With such structures we begin to do serious building comparable to the house. The quality of construction should be at least as good as that in the house; the same building code will apply to both. Some of these elements may be portions of the house opening to the garden, some of them may be built independently in the garden.

Often it is hard for us to say whether we are designing architectural or garden spaces. The overlapping of the two becomes very obvious with the introduction of these very useful and pleasant types of half-indoor, half-outdoor space. Each such closed shelter project seems to involve a special effort to resolve the contradictions between indoor and outdoor living. Therefore each problem must be specially analyzed, each solution specially programmed and designed for the individual family and site.

INDOOR-OUTDOOR PROBLEMS. Such solutions are bound to involve careful consideration of both indoor and outdoor problems. Questions to be answered will include:

1. How much cooking should you do indoors and how much out?
2. Do you need special dressing space, showers, or toilets for the new pool or game area?
3. Which of the children's toys should be kept indoors, which outdoors in the play yard?
4. Where do you put the garden furniture in bad weather?
5. How much can you extend the usefulness of the patio by keeping it warm, dry, and windfree, or by letting the breezes in without losing privacy, or by keeping insects out?

Materials and Utilities. Careful check of your utility connections may be necessary to determine the practicability of some of these projects. Materials for closed shelter construction are partly those used in open shelters, but largely those used in house construction. Wherever possible they should re-

Maynard L. Parker

Herrington-Olson

Ernest Braun

flect those used in your house. Usually these will be considered as buildings by the local building department. They will have to be built on concrete footings which prevent contact between wood and the earth, and will have to meet all other code requirements.

VINES AND STRUCTURES.   Planted shelter is of two kinds: vines on open structures, and trees. Vines are widely misunderstood and misused plants. They provide more show and interest from less ground space, and are more flexible in tight spaces, than any other plant forms. However, these possibilities can be realized only by careful study of the characteristics of the various kinds of vines.

1. How do they climb—by leaning, scrambling, matting, twining, or using tendrils, suckers, or claws?
2. How high will they climb?
3. How wide will they spread?
4. How thick and bushy will they become? (Or how much and how often will they require pruning?)
5. Are they deciduous or evergreen?
6. What color fruit or other special interest do they have?

Once these facts are known, we can design structures to suit specific vines, select vines to suit specific structures, or design both together to solve specific problems. For instance, wistaria will cover as much as an acre of ground, and is very long-lived; therefore it should be planted only on large strong structures which are expected to remain in place for many years. Star jasmine, on the other hand, will not climb much above 10 ft., and therefore is suited to modest structures and intimate scale.

Vines on open structures are intermediate in usefulness between structural shelters and trees. You get partial shelter sooner than with trees of economical size. The cost is less than that of more complete structural shelter, but more than that of ordinary trees. With deciduous vines you may get a more flexible shelter, if their dormant period coincides with the season in which you do not need shade. Old favorites, such as grapes, honeysuckle, wistaria, or climbing roses may be able to play a structural role in your garden. This is the most direct and balanced combination of the precision and order of good construction and the wayward charm of vegetation.

On the other hand, vines are very apt to be messy in tight spots, to build up mounds of dead wood which are very difficult to clear out, to rot, distort, or undermine construction, cause leaks in the roof, and so on. This is the reason for emphasizing the need for very careful study before a specific vine is planted on a specific structure.

Trees

Trees have been the friends of man ever since he first settled down on the land, providing him with shade and greenery, color and shelter, fruit and timber, and improving the local soil and climate in the process. We can scarcely add to the many rich words which have been spoken and written in appreciation of trees. Trees of all sizes and shapes, heavy or light, deciduous or evergreen, singly or in groups or groves, play a major sheltering role in our gardens and community landscapes.

The line between trees and shrubs is arbitrary, and there are many kinds which overlap it under varying conditions of growth. If we say that a tree is a plant which gets up high enough and spreads its branches widely enough for us to walk under them, we will find that there are single-trunked forms (as small flowering fruits or dwarf maples) which are not tall enough, or (as Lombardy poplars or Italian cypresses) broad enough to qualify. On the other hand there are many-stemmed forms—carobs, Katsura trees, olives, privets, crepe myrtle—which do. Many of these can be either shrub or tree form, depending on soil, moisture, pruning, and so on. There are many good small tree or semi-tree forms which are commonly forced into the role of shrubs, with inevitable distortions from crowding and trimming. Likewise there are good large shrub forms which are often distorted by training into unhappy imitations of trees.

Such distinctions come down to specific decisions with specific plants and gardening practices. Woody plants develop through juvenile, mature and aged forms. Many of them may pass from shrub to tree after the first or second of these. Thus the relation between shrub and tree forms is not so simple as the nursery catalogs or the botanical textbooks maintain. It is a question of spacing, based on understanding of the relation between ultimate size, form, and rate of growth of the specific plant. The distinction between trimming and pruning—which we will discuss under maintenance—is also important to this question.

OVERHEAD SHELTER. Definition of tree forms as those spreading foliage over our heads is a landscape classification, based on the function of plants in shaping our living spaces. Shrubs give enclosure at the *sides* of garden or park spaces, to any height, and with any degree of thickness or thinness. Trees give additional enclosure, or shelter, *overhead*. As Fitch says:

> The scientific use of . . . trees will accomplish any or all of the following:
> Deflect, absorb and reduce the heat radiation. . .
> Reduce the free air temperatures. . .

Filter the atmosphere. . .

Reduce intensities and glare. . .

Increase visual privacy. . .

Reduce the transmission of airborne sound. . . .

In general, trees have a stabilizing effect upon their immediate surroundings, reducing all environmental extremes. Rudolph Geiger, in his excellent study on the micro-climate, found that a mixed forest growth of spruce, oak, and poplar cuts off 69 per cent of the sun's heat from the ground. He found that forests are cooler in summer, warmer in winter than clear land; and that a belt of trees would reduce wind velocities by as much as 63 per cent. . . .

In the dry half of the country trees reduce the loss of moisture by reducing the drying effects of sun and wind, and increase humidity locally by transpiration (moisture given off from the leaves).

Deciduous trees have a specific functional value, in that they provide shade in the summer when it is needed, and let in the sun in winter when it is needed. This simple fact makes deciduous trees (sycamores, elms, maples) the most relevant large trees for use anywhere close to buildings, or over garden spaces which are to receive fairly intensive use. In the cooler northern half of the country, the space beneath the big evergreen trees, cool and breezy in the hot summer, becomes dank and forbidding during cold and wet winter months.

These statements must, however, be checked closely against your local climate. They are most true in those regions which have hot summers, cold winters, and intermediate springs and falls. Even there the period of dormancy or bareness of each specific kind of tree must be checked carefully against the season in which you want shade or no-shade. Deciduous trees are probably most useful in the northern half of the country and become less important as we move to milder winters and longer seasons. In the extreme South, shade the year round may be desirable.

HOW LARGE A TREE? Since even a small tree will become 15 to 20 ft. high and as much in spread, you should be very careful in your selection and placement of trees on the home grounds. This is especially true on the smaller lots on which most of us live. One ordinary shade tree of 30- to 50-ft. height and spread will dominate the average 50- to 60-ft. lot completely, leaving no room for variations in sun and shade. This may be all right if you are prepared to live with this one large tree, subordinating all your outdoor activities to it. Usually you should design the size and shape of tree you are planting as carefully as you would a structural shelter. The proportion of the

Union Pacific Railroad photo

House by Albert Henry Hill, architect; photo by Morley Baer

yard (front or back) which it will eventually cover must be visualized, and this should seldom be over 50 per cent.

This means, of course, that neighborhoods of small homes will tend to be neighborhoods of small trees, and the larger trees will be confined to streets, parks, and the grounds of institutions and larger residences. The only way for the resident of the average small home to guarantee regular experience of splendid, large trees (one of the rich experiences of life) is to participate in community programs aimed at bringing such planting close to his home, in public open spaces.

Tree Patterns. Since the average shade tree is a landscape element of about the same weight and importance as the average house, the average lot cannot contain more than one or two such trees. Great landscape patterns, such as we see in parks and rural countrysides, developed by combining many such trees of various kinds, can be developed in residential blocks only at the scale of the neighborhood, by street tree programs and neighborhood cooperation.

Organized spatial patterns can be developed on the private lot, however, through the use of tree forms that are tall but so narrow as to make little shelter (columnar trees, thin palms) or small tree forms less than 15 ft. high (8 ft. will shelter a man). These can be grouped closely enough (8 to 10 ft.) to use them in quantity (five to ten or more). Such quantities make possible organized patterns: architectural (rows which form enclosing planes) or irregular (scattered groups or small woods) or both together. This sort of planting, by combining the functions of enclosure and shelter in flexible patterns, makes richer and more interesting possibilities in the garden.

Shelter Decisions

The choice between structural or planted shelter, or what proportions or detailed kinds of each, must be based on careful analysis of the various aspects of the problem. As with enclosure, choice is best made through the development of a plan, based on this careful analysis, and putting the required elements together, in an imaginative and creative way, with the surfacing and enclosure elements. You must know:

1. What do you want to control by shelter—sun, rain, wind, snow, heat, glare, dust, noise, insects?
2. When do you want to control it (year-round or at certain seasons)?
3. Why do you want to control it? (Sometimes this is not clear.)
4. You must also know how much control is needed—100, 75, 50 per cent?

—or possible, and how soon. (Are you willing to wait three to five years for a tree to begin casting appreciable shade?) And then you must investigate relative costs of installing and maintaining various types of shelter, in relation to your own budget of money, material, and time.

5. Last, but definitely not least, you should have developed through your landscape plan certain esthetic principles: Are structures needed to supplement the house and extend it into the garden, or are trees needed to complement it and make a transition between the house and the surrounding landscape?

All of these factors have to be put together in a complicated equation from which should come the answer giving the right type or types of shelter for your garden. It would be nice to have an automatic calculator for such equations, but the closest we have is the plan. Better yet (or preceding it) may be the series of sketch plans exploring different systems and combinations of surfacing, enclosure, and shelter, until just the right one is found.

9. Enrichment

Enrichment is the furnishing or decoration of your garden rooms. The enrichment process provides facilities for sitting, eating, reading, playing, relaxing, sunbathing, and cooling off; it also makes the interiors of your garden rooms rich, warm, intimate, domestic, colorful, imaginative.

Quite often the exploration of these design possibilities will suggest uses and experiences in developed outdoor areas which otherwise might never have occurred to you. This exploration is accomplished by merging the best thinking in garden detailing, furniture and interior design, and art—painting, sculpture, ceramics, and related techniques.

There was a time when "enrichment" was a fighting word to the modern designer. He linked it with decoration and ornamentation, all of which he considered as futile efforts to apply beauty to the surface of something already completely designed. This was most true of the early modern architects of the "International Style." Frank Lloyd Wright never succumbed to the idea of the stripped-down building, and he has been the great enricher of twentieth century Western architecture, carrying the torch for the idea of richness organically designed into the structure of the building. Gradually the more extreme purist groups among the modern architects have moved in Wright's direction, moving from pure plaster, glass, and steel to the use of wood, masonry, and many other materials, colors, and textures. Today we have an American residential architecture which grows continuously warmer, more human, and more variable. This is affecting the allied arts also, to the point where we are beginning to see reasonably priced modern furniture which is both comfortable and good-looking.

Of course enrichment can become clutter and confusion, a hodge-podge which makes you nervous, irritable, and restless. This was the typical Victorian parlor, from which the pure early modern designers reacted so violently. It is just as important to design the total combination of enrichment elements in a harmonious and balanced pattern, as it is to design the surfacing, enclosing, and sheltering framework for them carefully.

Close perusal of any or all of the house, garden, and interior magazines today will prove that the same battle between good and bad design goes on constantly, regardless of slogans. In the twenties Victorian clutter was attacked by the pure-form-and-empty-space school; today the latter is being attacked as subversive by a so-called "free style" which at times almost gets back to the Victorian clutter. But through all of these wordy battles the esssential problem in the room or the garden remains to have just the right kind and quantity of enriching elements—not so much as to be cluttered, not so few as to seem barren.

ENRICHMENT ELEMENTS.   The elements of garden enrichment are many. They include garden elements, such as flowers and other small plants, ornamental water, rocks, driftwood, and other "found" art. They also include man-made elements, such as fixed and movable furniture, equipment such as barbecues and lighting fixtures, color by painting or staining, its refinement in wall or mural painting, mosaic, relief; sculpture, and other objects of art—ceramics, glass, metal, and so on.

All of these must be considered in relation to the possibilities for rich and interesting detailing in the primary surfacing, enclosure, and shelter elements. In other words, if you have a great interest in, or collection of, certain enriching materials (flowers, rocks) you may design your primary elements in a very plain and simple manner, in order to show off your main interest. On the other hand, if you anticipate no great interest in enrichment, you may want to put much more interest into the primary forms.

The two should never, of course, be completely separated in our thinking. Furniture, garden elements, and art forms can be integral, structural parts of surfacing, enclosure, and shelter, as our illustrations show. Their proper combination and arrangement require a combination of the talents of a good landscape architect and a good interior designer, even as the proper furnishing of the house requires the combination of architectural and interior design talents.

Plant Elements

Garden enrichment details include all of the traditional objects of gardening and horticultural interest which we have come to regard as central in the garden picture: annual beds, perennial borders, rose gardens, herb

Day
Lily

Cocks-
comb

Paul J. Peart

Petunias

Kassler Studios

Im-

Cosmos

Rose Hedda Hopper

Edwin T. Merchant; courtesy Howard & Smith

gardens, rock gardens, aquatics, succulents and cacti, bog gardens, vegetable gardens, shade gardens. These are developed for various reasons: for color, for cutting, for the kitchen, for collections, for interest in the plant and its setting, for horticultural activity such as propagating and hybridizing, for health and welfare and occupational therapy. Very often these garden details are developed for themselves alone, without adequate regard for setting, background, or framing. Yet even if they are your one and only interest in the garden, they will show up better and give you more returns for your effort in a proper frame of the three primary elements. On the other hand, if you are primarily interested in outdoor living space, but want to enrich it with a little dabbling in garden details, they can be made a flexible and not too ostentatious part of the whole scheme.

These garden details are useful but not essential to the enrichment of the outdoor living room. If you like some or all of them, and want to take care of them, have them. On the other hand, you can have a rich and interesting garden without any of them. Note the remarks on color and maintenance in Chapter 10, "Plants and Planting."

The herbaceous border, in which annuals, perennials, and bulbs are grown in various, more or less changing combinations, is the rich and fine peak of flower gardening skill.

Flower gardening is very rewarding for those who take an active interest in it. Nothing is lovelier than a well-planned and well-grown border. Endless variation in changing and experimenting with various combinations and new plantings is possible at little cost except in personal time and energy.

Climate has a great deal to do with successful flower gardening. The mild and humid climate of England made her the originator of the herbaceous border idea, and she is still a leader in it. Climates which are more extreme in their combinations of heat, cold, moisture, or dryness—as are most climates in the United States—are likewise more difficult for flower gardening. However, it is only in the extreme North Center, Southeast, and Southwest that this difficulty grows so great as to seriously inhibit flower growing in the private garden.

Setting should also be considered in planning flower beds. The herbaceous border always shows off best when it has a strong and solid background of structure or green planting, and when it is so framed in the garden pattern as to be an essential and indispensable part of it. All of these remarks apply also to vegetable gardens if they are grown for ornament as well as utility. This is perfectly proper and possible, as the forms and colors of most vegetables are very rich and interesting in themselves.

Annuals (including those bulbs which have to be lifted and replanted each year) are the easiest and quickest source of color in house and garden.

However they also require most care, since their beds must be changed each year. This attention may not be too much trouble when the annuals are grown for cutting, in a service or utility garden. But when they are grown for color in the main garden area, in beds which should look well all the time, it requires very careful planning and skillful gardening to achieve continuous good results with these short-lived plants.

Biennials, which live two years, and perennials (including permanent bulbs) which live three or more years without disturbance, give greater results for less continuous effort. All of these flowering plants require careful preparation of the soil before they are planted. There are great variations in perennial culture, from those which must be lifted and divided every two or three years, to those which can stay in the ground undisturbed for long periods of time.

The other types of special color or interest planting—roses; herbs, alpines, succulents and cacti; aquatics and bog plants; shade plants—are all more permanent, durable, and steady in effect. With proper soil preparation and growing conditions, they will persist and improve for many years.

Roses, perhaps the prime favorite of most American gardeners, will grow well in all parts of the country, if the right varieties are selected. While the flowers are lovely, few hybrid roses are very interesting in form or foliage. Therefore the successful rose garden frames the roses in beds with boxwood hedges, edging plants, or structural curbs; it places these beds in organized patterns dominated by special features such as ornamental pools, arbors with seats, birdbaths, sundials, or other sculptural elements. All of these features and patterns—whether "traditional" or "modern"—function to frame and show off the loveliness of the rose flower while compensating for the inadequacies of the rose plant.

Of course there are some who say that roses should not be grown in areas visible in the main garden, but only in rows in the utility area, for cutting and display in the house. Some types of roses—polyanthus, floribundas, grandifloras, and old-fashioned species—are sufficiently shrubby and well formed to combine well with other types of shrubs. The hybrid types are generally more demanding in culture—requiring special feeding, watering, spraying, and dusting—than these shrubby types.

Herbs, alpines, succulents, and cacti are similar in that most of them require sharp drainage for success. This means that they are best grown in raised beds or containers of very sandy or porous soil, unless the natural soil has those qualities. They are useful in dry walls, rocky banks, and similar situations which are bad for more moisture-loving plants. Alpines, being from higher elevations, seem to do better in the northern half of the country, where the humidity is neither too low nor too high. Succulents and cacti,

Succulents and cacti

William Aplin; courtesy Sunset

on the other hand, are in general quite sensitive to frost, which limits them to the southern half, and to excess moisture, which in turn limits them to the Southwest for any use more general than dish gardening. Succulents (leaf succulents) are adapted to semiarid or subhumid climates, and few will take the extreme conditions of the true desert, where cacti (stem succulents) are at home. Even in the desert there are variations. Some cacti which are at home in the Arizona desert will only grow in shade in the Coachella Valley in California. Herbs of many kinds are of course generally adaptable throughout our country.

Aquatics and bog plants, which of course require constant excess moisture, are useful wherever ponds, streams, or swampy areas occur naturally or are created artificially. In the humid East they are more abundant in nature, and this tends to make them more generally accepted and used in gardens. In the arid West they are apt to be associated with a more artificial or stylized use of water, in small quantities and special positions.

These plants also have their special cultural requirements, varying from the pure floating water plants through those which like to root into a dirt bottom to the bog plants, which are marginal between water and land. The special project involved in producing a balance of plant and animal life in the ornamental lily or fish pool has its own special fascination.

Shade planting is useful and interesting where shade exists naturally—as under heavy trees, or on the north sides of buildings, or steep slopes. You may also create shade conditions artificially, by planting trees or by building structures such as lath houses. You may do this because you are interested in growing and collecting shade-loving plants, or because you feel the need of modifying a climate which is oppressively hot at certain seasons of the year. Such seasons occur throughout our country, except on the extreme Northwest coast.

There are many kinds of plants which require partial shade for best growth. Most typically they like the filtered light produced by tree tops or lath houses. This is shade gardening at its best. Heavier shade, or the strong alternations of the east and west sides of buildings, require more careful selection among hardier plants.

Plants for shade gardening include ferns, begonias, fuchsias, camellias, rhododendrons, azaleas, many small cover plants, and the bewildering profusion of tropical foliage plants popular in the extreme southern portions of the United States and in the Hawaiian Islands.

Many of these, as camellias and azaleas, require very good drainage, provided by sand in the soil and porous rock beneath if necessary. Most of them require constant moisture in the soil; many in the air as well. The majority require soil somewhat acid in reaction, similar to their natural forest condi-

Paul J. Peart

Shade plants

Paul J. Peart

William Aplin

tions. This can of course be provided with peat moss and acid soil conditions.

While the shade garden is delightful in warm weather, it should be located carefully in relation to living spaces and the source of shade. It should not cut off sun from house or patio when it is needed during cool seasons. Some trees are apt to be damaged by constant moisture too close to their trunks.

All of these specialized garden plants have their own special cultural requirements and problems, and these vary from region to region throughout the country. The general requirements are well summarized in books such as Gardner's BASIC HORTICULTURE. Beyond that it is usually best to consult local authorities and experience for a choice among these special garden elements, or for the proper way to grow any one of them. There are national societies for those interested in most specialized plants—roses, chrysanthemums, begonias, ferns, and succulents, to name a few—and their local chapters will be most interested in helping you.

Local possibilities and personal interest will influence your choice among these special garden plants for enrichment purposes. Sometimes certain questions of suitability and compatibility may arise. For instance in some mild regions we may be able to grow both succulents and shade plants by creating proper conditions. Some will argue that in a semiarid climate the shade plants, particularly of a more tropical type, are inappropriate and should be avoided in favor of succulents and drought-resistant shrubs and herbs. Others will argue that these only accentuate the more extreme conditions of heat and low humidity, whereas shade gardening will moderate these and produce a more balanced and comfortable living condition.

These arguments may be reversed in mild humid regions. All of these arguments—or similar debates which may occur in other parts of the country—have convincing elements in them. No generalized rules on such questions are possible—each reader must reach his or her own decision on the basis of their own needs, desires, and ideas. But we must emphasize that whether you use planting that is native or similar to it, planting that is from more extreme climates than your own (like cactus) or planting that is from less extreme climates than your own (like tropicals) successful design is based on creating the proper framing conditions immediately around the special planting, and the proper transition—not too crude, abrupt, or obvious—to the general conditions in the immediate neighborhood. It is abrupt changes and unplanned contrasts between entirely different kinds of planting that are most disturbing.

In addition to special plantings, garden enrichment elements include ornamental water, rocks, driftwood, and other "found art," and most certainly birds and animals. Each of these has special properties as a design material.

Water

The character of water, the most plastic and receptive of our materials, is determined by the character of its container, and by the rate and direction of movement we give it. It seeks always a level plane surface, expressing the pull of gravity and, when at rest, complete balanced stability. It is also affected by its chemical, plant, or animal content: it tends to breed life (algae and mosquitos) as it has throughout geologic history, unless specifically prevented from doing so.

We tend to use water in our gardens in more humid climates because its more or less constant presence as natural surface water makes it more or less an automatic part of our design vocabulary; and in more arid climates because its importance to comfort and to life receives extra emphasis there. In terms of increasing the livability of our homes, water is most relevant in hot arid climates and least in cool humid climates. In the former, water is the final touch which makes the garden livable; in the latter it is apt to be merely boring. It is the moistness of water which makes it relevant as aridity increases, and the coolness which makes it important as heat increases.

Water has a number of other qualities that are directly relevant to its use in the garden. These include quietude, repose, depth, tension, or solidity. Its range of reflective qualities is shown by the contrast between still water in large or deep basins with dark linings, and the lightness and sparkle of moving water in shallow basins with light linings. The possibilities for putting water in motion give the designer control of a sort of dance chorus, with its own trickling or splashing sound accompaniment. The range is from the graceful sparkle of the single jet to the solid power of the heavy waterfall.

Water not only derives part of its character from the materials lining its container, but such materials, under a thin film of water, double their quality and attraction. Brick and tile, glazed or unglazed; sand, pebbles, stone, concrete; plants and animals; all receive an exaggerated emphasis in color and texture when wet. Water also functions as a bounding or blocking element in the organization of garden space, because one must walk around it, rather than through it. It is as effective as a low hedge or wall in blocking physical, but not visual, movement. This has been discussed in Chapter 7, on enclosure, along with the types of containers for water in the garden. There is no clear line between water used for enclosure and for enrichment.

SWIMMING POOLS. In the average garden swimming pools require very careful treatment because they are such big holes in the ground. Otherwise they become out of scale with the garden, swallow it up, and destroy its spacious quality. This, of course, may not be too big a price to pay for the morning dip and the afternoon plunge. But it is usually possible to design the pool-garden relation so that both the pleasure of the water and the quality of the garden are improved rather than depreciated. The primary principle for achieving this is very simple: the garden must shape the pool, rather than being forced to conform to it. While serious swimming and diving demand specific rectangular proportions in plan form, and specific relations of deep to shallow in section, few private pools are used so seriously as to limit them to that purely functional form. The standardized shapes offered by swimming pool companies (the rectangle, the decorated rectangle, the oval, the kidney bean) are merely substitutes for integrated design of garden including pool.

The Gunite system, developed in California, has been largely responsible for the lower costs, and consequently increased market, that have recently been achieved in pool construction. This system is cheaper and more efficient than any of the other methods—stone, concrete block, steel, poured or dry-packed concrete. It requires very careful attention to the form of the excavation, the character of the soil, and to surface and subsurface drainage. This makes it possible for the soil to carry part of the load which is carried entirely by the structure in the other systems. Carefully engineered reinforcing is placed by hand against the excavation, and the wet concrete is blown in place under high pressure.

Adequate equipment for the pool includes primarily the filter system, which keeps the water clearer and the pool cleaner. Tank, pump, and pipe sizes must all be properly engineered to the size of the pool. Provision must be made for backwashing the filters, for cleaning the pool regularly, for skimming floating material from the water, for chlorinating the water, and for reducing alkalinity, iron, and scale-forming hardness. Once the equipment is in, the pool must be serviced regularly every month. This service can be hired for $25 to $30 per month. Your utility bills may run another $20 to $25 per month higher, especially if you have a heater.

Pool enclosure must also be considered. The social responsibilities which come with the ownership of a swimming pool cannot be minimized, and greatest of these is the necessity for supervising children while in or near the pool, and of keeping them out when such supervision is not available. Too many children have drowned in unsupervised pools. The chain-link fence around the pool, as the simplest solution to this control problem, usually spoils both pool and garden by cutting up the space of the garden, and by creating an obvious barrier between house, patio, and pool. This is most true, of course, in the small yard, where the pool must be close to the house. More space makes possible more freedom in fencing and yard division.

Pool designed by Samuel Marx, architect; photo by Julius Shulman; courtesy Condé Nast

Morley Baer

It may be possible to design special fence patterns or alignments which will minimize the division of garden space and still cut off the pool. But this has to be worked out before the pool is built, not after. A possible substitute for fencing is the plastic cover which is cut to fit the pool exactly, rolls out horizontally to cover the water and float on it, and is fastened to hooks along the sides. This problem of enclosing the pool without spoiling it is worthy of considerable study, and should not be approached carelessly at the last minute.

Relations with your friends may present another problem of pool ownership—less critical and yet more exasperating. Casual acquaintances suddenly become bosom pals, and arrive every Sunday to spend the afternoon in the pool. Old friends who lack the brass to walk in without invitation may gradually drop out of your life under this new kind of pressure. The pitiful appeals of the neighborhood children on hot days may leave you, unless your heart is very hard, as their unpaid recreation supervisor. This kind of problem may appear unimportant to many readers, who will have their own special solutions for it.

Financing of swimming pools can now be done in the same way as home improvements along with various other miscellaneous additions to house and garden. However, it should be clear that the problem is not merely one of getting the pool built, with or without enclosure.

Maintenance is a steady burden, and the social problems may prove difficult. While the private pool in one's own backyard is a delightful luxury, careful analysis may lead one to co-operate with the neighbors in promoting jointly a pool convenient for all. This can be accomplished through the machinery of local government or private association.

Rock

Rock has been used as an enriching element in the garden in many ways and places. You will have noted our remarks about its sculptural use at large scale for partial enclosure. We have also mentioned that the best prototypes for such rockwork seem to exist in the Orient. This does not imply that many very fine examples of sensitive rock arrangement cannot be found in America and Europe, for they certainly can. However, the tradition has existed on a mass scale for many centuries in China and Japan. The refinement in rockwork which occurs generally there occurs only individually here.

The sculptural use of rocks for enrichment purposes may be defined as one in which the individual rocks are carefully arranged and separated from one another, with space between. This implies that the rocks are carefully selected for their special interest in form, texture, and color. The objective of such arrangements is to show off these interesting qualities, and in doing it to establish special relations between the various rocks, so that each is helped by the others around it. Thus one vertical rock may be shown off among several horizontal rocks; one red rock among several white or black ones; and so on. While such groupings may have content of sentimental, symbolic, or scientific nature, the expression of that content will be strengthened, and the appeal of the grouping widened, by strong clear arrangement. These relations are developed by the application of the general design principles of unity and variety, interest and harmony, dominance and contrast, rhythm and balance.

In addition to the larger-scale enclosing arrangements previously mentioned, this analysis of rock arrangements as sculptural groupings is important to the design of: rock gardens, for alpines or succulents; "Oriental" or "naturalistic" rock arrangements; the geologic or tourist collection; combination with actual sculpture to provide a good setting for it. Sculpture by carving is of course the ultimate refinement of rock.

Other Natural Materials

Other natural materials may be used, although plants and rocks have long been the most popular for garden enrichment. In recent years various kinds of "found" or "accidental" art have been used. Weathered wood fragments of all sorts, from beach or mountain, and including branches, trunks, and stumps as well as pieces of processed lumber if strongly weathered, have been used in a decorative or sculptural way, usually in combination with plants and rocks. Such material is very interesting, but it must be carefully selected, arranged, and installed to be completely convincing, and to "wear well" with the observer for any length of time. The same applies to various other miscellaneous objects of interest, such as bones or fragments of man-made objects or construction.

ANIMALS. If plants are the primary framework of landscape design, animals are one of its major enrichments. They are important elements in the natural and rural landscape, and they are certainly important to every homeowner and farmer who may keep them as pets or as a source of income. While there are obvious contradictions between certain animals and certain types of gardening—some dogs dig up the grass and flowers—these can be solved by careful design.

Rock garden designed by Nagao Sakurai; photo by Garrett Eckbo

Wherever possible, animals around the home should be made a part of the landscape scheme as an additional enriching element, rather than hidden away in a special yard. Think for a moment of the black Scottie, the red Irish setter, the spotted Dalmatian; Siamese and Persian cats; the flash and sparkle of aviaries; fine saddle horses, muscled work horses, golden Palominos; the pheasant, the rooster, the guinea hen, the swan; goldfish and frogs and dragonflies. Well-to-do farms and estates have developed many interesting ideas for the integration of animals with the designed landscape. The public zoo is of course the most obvious example of the use of animals in a public landscape. Progress in zoo design has been in the direction of incorporating animals in a more carefully designed and natural-seeming landscape.

Shelters are an essential part of the problem of using animals constructively in the garden. Dog houses, chicken houses, fish pools, and stables can all be designed as attractive elements in the landscape, rather than allowed to be accidental eyesores.

Man-Made Elements

Garden enrichment made by man includes furniture and equipment, color by paint or stain, sculpture and other objects of art. Of these the first are essential to the livability of the garden, and nearly always appear in some form. Color may appear as a finish for wood or other materials but seldom in any more obviously artistic use. Sculpture and other such objects are rare, doubtless because of the poverty-stricken character of most of those available to the average pocketbook.

The furnishing of the patio, terrace, or other outdoor living and dining space has problems parallel to, though usually simpler than, those of furnishing the living portions of the house. We need places to sit or lie down in sun or shade; occasional tables on which to set food, drinks, reading matter, or tobacco; storage for furniture and incidentals; some free area for standing, walking around, or dancing; good light for night use; attention to acoustics and ventilation.

The basic elements of living spaces are outlined by Robert Woods Kennedy in his book THE HOUSE. As he says, outdoor living is an expansion of indoor, hence less complex. It may become almost equally complex with sufficient interest, especially in the warmer regions where its season is longer. Kennedy points out the importance of creating an atmosphere expressive of the owner's taste and social standing; of a source of fire as a focus for social grouping; of creating proper settings for conversation (an

William Aplin

Robert Royston

Morley Baer; courtesy House Beautiful

art as well as a pastime); of a source of music, with easy control; of the fact that some people like to sit against a wall or in a corner, while others like to sit in the open; and of making a living space a dead-end area, without circulation, and with the possibility of closing it off from children's play or other distractions.

All of these elements can assume equal importance in the outdoor living space, if it is developed to its maximum potential. Most of them must be determined and solved at the planning stage, and are controlled by the entire process of selecting and combining surfacing, enclosure, shelter, and enrichment.

GARDEN FURNITURE. Seats and tables and other garden furniture may be either fixed or movable. This choice is comparable to that offered to the owners of many modern houses in their selection of interior furniture.

Fixed furniture is designed and built with the basic enclosure and shelter elements of the garden. As part of the permanent design framework, it is somewhat more efficient than movable furniture, in that it serves people while also helping to give over-all form to the garden. It also takes up less space than movable furniture. On the other hand it does not have the flexibility of the latter, and may not be as comfortable unless equipped with movable elements such as seat pads.

Fixed furniture must stand all weather, so must be designed and built more durably than the movable types, which can be stored for the winter. Fixed furniture can be designed to accommodate more people comfortably in the same space than any collection of movable pieces. However, movable pieces, specially designed for quantity production in shops, can be made more subtle and comfortable in form. On-site techniques are generally more limited, because they are more expensive than shop techniques.

Most ready-made garden furniture is clumsy if not actually ugly in appearance, although it may be comfortable. The design talents brought to bear on it have seldom—with a few notable exceptions—been comparable to those applied to indoor furniture. Wood furniture, especially of redwood, assumes clumsy and elephantine proportions, apparently expressing both rusticity and durability. Metal furniture, while lighter, is apt to be ungraceful, hard, and sterile in appearance. Covers and cushions are given the hard and gaudy colors of store awnings and auto seat cushions. The general theory seems to be that outdoor furniture, since it is "only" for the garden, need have no grace or charm. If any particular quality is needed it can be either rustic or gaudy, since these can be produced without the extra expense of the good designer. The few notable exceptions to this general low level of garden furniture have included pieces designed by Van Keppel-Green, Hardoy, and Royston.

Seats and lounges whether fixed or movable must have proper heights and angles of seats and backs for active sitting, as when eating; more relaxed sitting as when talking or reading; and actual lounging or napping, in sun or shade. These three different types of seating should be part of the basic garden plan.

Tables also require three useful heights: 14 in. for coffee tables, 18 in. for benches and serving tables, 28½ in. for dining and working.

The basic furniture materials are of course wood or metal. The choice between them is one of design—do we want furniture of a warm and solid quality, or should it be light and graceful? Pads, seats, or backs may be of canvas, plastic, or cord. All of these are nondurable materials which require replacement every few years. Colors should be very carefully selected. White or black are most reliable, if you have any doubts. Glass-topped tables are as elegant in the patio as in the living room.

Furniture storage must be considered even in the mildest climates. Movable garden furniture is best stored under shelter during rainy weather, and this means a special structure, shed, or wide overhang on the house roof. Stored furniture is bulky and unpleasant to see from the house. It may be put in an inconspicuous corner of the garden shelter, or in a special shed or part of the garage. In sections where wet and dry seasons are definitely separated, we may not mind moving the furniture to a special spot for the three or four rainy months of the year. (Of course in a dry winter we may haul them out again.) In sections with rainy summers a rainproof section of garden shelter, or house roof overhang, should be handy for quick protection during showers and storms.

LIGHTING. Garden lighting is a refined and intimate problem, whose possibilities have to be explored both practically and romantically. The problem arises partly from the desire to use the garden at night, and partly from the increasing use of glass in our houses. The close union of house and garden which large glass areas accomplish during the day has certain strange contradictions at night. Without light outside the glass becomes a mirror, reflecting accurately everything inside. This is usually quite an uncomfortable experience, for which there are only two solutions. We can put in drapes, and pull them every dark night (often to the great annoyance of the architect). Or we can install garden lighting of approximately the same intensity as the indoor lighting. This will maintain the same visual continuity from inside to outside as we have during the day.

The practical problems of garden lighting are those of giving light where it is needed, at the right strength, without at any time shining it directly into the eyes of people in the garden, and in places to which conduits can

Julius Shulman

Ernest Braun

Robert Royston

be run inconspicuously and with least expense. The usual spotlights and floodlights placed on the eaves or walls of the house are no solution for garden use. They merely make it unpleasant to go out at night. Light has to be made indirect, either by screening the source with structure or planting, or by enclosing it in frosted glass, plastic, canvas, or other diffusing medium.

There may, of course, be a special security system of floodlights, controlled by one master switch beside the bed, for use if one hears prowlers at night. But this purpose is the reverse of lighting for use and beauty. It is intended to make intruders uncomfortable, and should therefore be a separate system. Lighting patio or terrace for use at night is comparable to lighting the living room. We need general illumination, built into the top or sides of the enclosing structure. And we need special illumination for special spots where we may want to read, cook, or play games.

Lighting for pictorial effect as viewed from house or terrace is a different and more complex problem. The romantic possibilities are dramatic in the highest degree: the spotlighting of special plants, the silhouetting of trees and shrubs, the bringing out of special colors, the use of various colored lights, the control of light horizontally or vertically in quite precise forms, light through glass and water. Outdoor lighting is apt to be expensive and technically complicated, but full of great possibilities for spatial drama in the night. It usually involves the extension of electric conduit to the periphery or boundaries of the garden area, and the establishment of lights or outlets in the tops of trees or in the ground below them, before or behind selected groups of trees or shrubs, before flower beds, in the bottom or sides of pools, near special objects of art, and so on.

Restraint should always be exercised in garden lighting. These effects are subject to considerable ingenuity in placement, single or multiple switching, and other refinements, but it is best not to go so far as to create an obvious display of cleverness. Restraint on the side of simplicity is likely to be more successful. We must also think about what the fixtures will look like in the daylight. It is always disconcerting to discover that the source of that midnight glamour is a couple of ugly mechanical floodlights partially screened by a pair of frowzy shrubs in the middle of the lawn. There are times when much extension of conduits can be saved by the use of something as simple as the Hawaiian torch—a metal holder on a pole, in which burns a cloth soaked in kerosene. Pictorial lighting can also, of course, function to light the garden for circulation at night.

ACOUSTICS AND VENTILATION. Sound and air are factors best controlled by enclosure and shelter elements. The softening of interior sounds is not a serious problem in the average garden, which includes a good deal of planting and many rough or broken surfaces. Exclusion of outside noise may be a serious problem. It can be reduced by high solid construction or dense thick planting. Ventilation requires careful analysis. Do we want to invite breezes in, keep wind out, or do both at different times? Structure and planting can be designed accordingly.

FIRE. The fireplace can be a focal point in patio or terrace as in the living room. In its simplest form it can be a masonry circle built into grass or paving, or a raised metal brazier filled with glowing coals.

The more elaborate barbecue-fireplace in permanent masonry must be approached with great care. It is heavy, monumental, and obtrusive, and is apt to take over the garden picture and destroy its scale and sense of space unless very carefully handled. You should first be sure that the simple fire circle or brazier is inadequate for outdoor warmth, and that the portable barbecue is not best for outdoor cooking. Then, if a more elaborate structure is required, it should be designed very carefully, simply, and functionally, as part of the enclosing structure if possible. Once built, this masonry structure will be extremely difficult to remove. Not only its detailed form, but its exact position in relation to house and patio should be carefully studied.

For many families the best thing about outdoor cooking is that it removes the grease of frying and broiling from the kitchen. For this purpose it can be installed just outside the kitchen, in the service yard. All of which is not to say that cooking and eating outdoors in your own garden may not be one of your most recreative activities.

OTHER ENRICHMENT ELEMENTS. Outdoor music may be supplied (if the neighbors don't mind) by conveniently placed speakers from high quality equipment indoors, or by portable radios and phonographs. Control of the former may be inconvenient, although with several long-playing records a nonstop program of some length is now possible.

The other factors which add up to the atmosphere of patio and living room, or both combined—arrangements to promote relaxing or constructive conversation, secure seating against walls, and airy seating in the open, the elimination of through circulation and the possibility of closing off distracting play activities nearby—are all elements involved in the general planning of the patio. These must be established before the detailed selection of furnishing and other objects begins.

EQUIPMENT. Yard equipment can become surprisingly complex and difficult, even in the average garden. It may perhaps be argued whether

Morley Baer

Mason Weymouth; courtesy Better Homes & Gardens

Photo by Julius Shulman; copyright Condé
Nast Publications, Inc.

barbecue-fireplaces and lights are furniture or equipment. As we go beyond those we begin to take in the entire area of garden or lot, rather than primarily the patio or terrace. In the front yard even such simple elements as mail box and street number, if not attached directly to the house, may spoil the approach to the house if carelessly placed.

THE SERVICE AREA. Clotheslines, garbage and trash cans, and incinerator are the orphans of most residential development. No one thinks of them before the house is built, and often not until the family moves in. Then they are placed hastily, and perhaps too prominently. The landscape architect is often approached quietly by neighbors of his clients, who in careful whispers ask him if he can't do something to hide those *awful* clotheslines.

Secluded in the service yard which is planned for it this equipment can be straightforward and functional. How many feet of line does your family need? In a tree, a removable reel, or stationary tees? Adequate size and space are the primary requisites to keeping all such service facilities useful and clean. Some people feel that, with a combination of automatic dryer in the house and regular trash and garbage collection services, the service yard can be dispensed with entirely. This may be true for small families or exceptionally neat housekeepers. But the average family is still likely to need a place to air out the bedding, store trash until collection time, store firewood, broken toys, building materials, and all the other miscellaneous messy things that are apt to accumulate around the home.

Special work spaces. In providing service areas one may find it necessary to expand into all sorts of more specialized work spaces, up to and including the ultimate functionalism of farm structures and farmyards. (All of the material in this book is aimed at the farm dweller just as much as at the urbanite with the small yard.) Special work space is necessary for the active gardener, who needs benches for potting and propagating; bins for fertilizers, topsoil, leaf mould, and peat moss; shelf storage for sprays, dusts, seeds, and small tools; glass houses and lath houses. Even the smallest garden with least maintenance will need a convenient storage space for a few garden tools. The home handyman or craftswoman will need adequate workspace, shelter, and facilities, including storage for tools and materials.

Every home needs adequate outdoor storage space for tools, material, play equipment, outdoor furniture, and all the other miscellaneous impedimenta which it tends to accumulate. The outdoor storage wall has become as well established as its indoor prototype, combining as it does functional enclosure with useful protected space.

PLAY EQUIPMENT. Recreation equipment becomes important as we expand our thinking from patio, terrace, and workspace to the larger garden with open lawn, which begins to take on some of the qualities of park or playground. Many of us desire these qualities in our own home grounds because they are so scarce or difficult to reach in our neighborhood or community. "A park and playground in every backyard" might be a good slogan for a city planner who has political ambitions. This slogan could take on physical reality if park systems were expanded and subdivisions rearranged so that every lot backed up to a finger of park space (instead of an alley) which connected directly with larger park and playground facilities. Until such things begin to happen, most of us will continue to make the most of the private lot space we have.

In terms of active play, provision for recreation includes a great variety of specific field and court spaces, equipment and apparatus, and such special elements as swimming pools (already discussed). In the average home one might find play space with apparatus and sand box for small children, perhaps a badminton or paddle tennis court on lawn or blacktop, a single basketball backstop, a ping-pong table in the patio, horseshoes or croquet, occasionally a small swimming pool.

All of these have their special design problems. Children's play space will be outgrown in five or six years, unless new ones come along to keep it in use. Such spaces should be convertible to other uses once they are outgrown. Games on the lawn make no visual problem until they begin to wear out the grass. But blacktop areas for games may be unsightly unless very carefully designed into the general garden pattern. Sometimes garage court or guest parking space can double as play space. The ping-pong table is furniture which is theoretically demountable, but because of its size is more apt to be left standing. Therefore it should have a special area to itself.

Color

Garden color is thought of as coming primarily from flowers, fruit, or autumn foliage. Yet synthetic color in the form of paints or stains is usually present in the house or other structures, and can be very useful in the garden picture. This is a special and complex field of design. It has been explored with considerable thoroughness by painters, interior designers, industrial designers, advertising men, sales managers, industrial engineers, psychologists, architects, and so on. And yet the general physical habitat of the American people, even at its more comfortable levels, is strangely bare of color; strangely dull, flat, neutral, barren, grayed or pastelled. The fear of color

Art in the Garden

1. Garden wall in tile mosaic by Roberto Burle Marx; colors blue, brown, gray, Venetian red, yellow
2. Sculptured panel in concrete and iron by Florence Swift

Marcel Gautherot

1.

Ernest Braun

2.

which seems so evident in outdoor "design in good taste" is perhaps a reaction and shrinking from those color orgies perpetrated by advertising and commercial design. Yet since the days of ancient Greece and China, clear, bright, strong colors have been used freely by great cultures. We need not fear them, but rather should learn to use them with care.

The two principal problems involved in the use of pure synthetic color in the garden are:

1. To what surfaces do we apply it?
2. How do we combine it with the colors of vegetation, earth, rock, and natural or unfinished materials?

Painted surfaces require maintenance; they must be repainted regularly. Wood, brick, stone, or concrete, if they will take the weather without protection, are probably best left natural. This has been the thesis of many modern architects. However, paints also are improving in quality. We should not hesitate to paint any of these surfaces if we are convinced that it will improve the general scheme. But we must be very sure before we cover up the natural beauty of such materials.

Stucco, which has no character in itself, is a more natural vehicle for color by paint. If, in our original design, we can project a pattern of natural surfaces and colored surfaces, these latter might well be of stucco. Other sheet materials—plywood, hardboard, asbestos-cement—are also good surfaces for color by paint.

Colored stains provide one bridge between the need for color and the desire to save the surface quality of wood or concrete. These soak in rather than seal the surface, and give color without changing the texture of concrete, or destroying the grain pattern of the wood.

Color choice may present problems. Much paint color is apt to seem harsh in the garden; a little trim color, on fence cap or bench, will go a long way. Green paint is most difficult to combine with vegetation; it seems to kill the natural greens. Blue is also difficult, or any color that is harsh or muddy. Clear, light, warm earth colors are best with green vegetation. With sufficient study and control we can find foliage to combine with any paint color, but the problem is apt to become too complex for ordinary procedures. We have to examine not only the color and texture of wall and plants, but the quality of atmosphere and light peculiar to the region in which we are working, and the orientation of the wall. For instance, gray foliage is handsome against a black wall, but only a few gray plants will do well on an east exposure, and almost none against a wall facing north.

MURAL PAINTING. The ultimate refinement of the use of pigment in the landscape is the painting applied directly to a structural wall. Mural painting, fresco or otherwise, seems somewhat foreign and strange to us—an art lost since the Renaissance, and now a startling intrusion into our quiet gardens. But the art has remained alive, and has indeed passed through a new renaissance in Mexico. Sooner or later it will have a similar renaissance with us. It is natural for people to decorate walls with paintings; for thousands of years paintings were done only on walls. The detached easel painting is less than 500 years old. This is a short time historically.

As soon as we apply two or more colors to a single wall panel, thereby producing a pattern of some sort, we are entering the field of mural painting. Of course it is a long way from there to the great works of history, or of our contemporaries in Mexico. Mural or wall painting is a serious professional project. This means that any amateur must be prepared to undertake serious and prolonged study before attempting it. But all artists are amateurs at some time in their beginnings. Any amateur who takes the possibilities seriously can by study learn enough either to attempt a painting himself or to enlist the aid of a professional. Few professional painters actually earn their living by painting.

Abstraction or Representation. The argument resulting from the modern movement in art will trouble any serious student. Without entering into involved discussion, we might say that pure abstraction and pure representation are both extreme forms of painting. The bulk of the work done now, as well as all through history, falls between these extremes. Most art has always tried to represent known subjects, and most art has simplified, distorted, or abstracted those subjects in some way in the interest of better form in the painting. So you should not be afraid of the logical extremes to which no painter need ever go, nor should you be afraid of the labels which zealous debaters persist in applying to every painting. The main test of each painting is how good, rich, or full an experience it gives those who view it. But in order to apply this test to paintings in a fair and reasonable way the viewers must approach them with open minds, without preconceptions as to what a painting should or should not be, but merely in search of a new way of looking at the world.

What has all this to do with color on your garden walls? Only that, once we begin to use color on vertical surfaces, an endless series of possibilities opens up, culminating in mature and full-grown mural painting. You don't, of course, have to explore all those possibilities in your own backyard. You may only go a few steps along the way: a decorative pattern of two or three colors, perhaps a more clever abstraction which gives a sense of space, perhaps a touch of surrealism with hands and feet without bodies. Whatever exploration of the uses of color on wall surfaces you may try, with or without more professional help, it will be more rewarding the more you know about

the general subject of painting: its past, present, and future; its potentials
and dangers.

MOSAIC. Painting, rich and varied though it be, is only one of the mani-
fold possibilities for garden enrichment which the world of art offers. Although the finished painting may convey great illusions of depth and
three-dimensional figures, it is nevertheless a liquid applied to a flat surface.
Unless it is done quite skillfully it is apt to seem contrived and unsatisfactory.
Elements which have a material quality and a third dimension of their own
may prove more satisfactory. Rich and interesting work can be done with
mosaic: patterns made with small bits of stone, glass, marble, or tile. Mosaic
merges with regular glazed tile work, units 4 by 4 inches or larger, highly
developed in Spain, Portugal, and Latin America, and quite successfully developed in the United States. These are flat patterns, much less subtle than
painting, but with a greater sense of being part of the structure to which
they are applied.

RELIEF. Art develops an actual third dimension with relief work, in
which by carving, forming, or setting blocks, some portions of the wall
surface are brought forward while others recede. Historically relief carving
has been an important part of architectural decoration, lending a special
realistic quality to otherwise flat panels. It is one of the simplest ways to
integrate sculpture with structure.

Art is always more convincing if it is an apparently necessary part of a
necessary structure. One of the great problems of the easel painting is to find
a wall on which it seems to belong. In gardens we begin to play with the idea
of relief on a wall when we set some units forward and some back in a wall
of brick, concrete block, or stone. Very interesting patterns can be produced
with this simple technique. Stucco is, of course, a material which lends itself
to a great deal of surface modeling and forming. As we go from these to the
more subtle work of the serious professional artist, we may obtain prefabricated relief panels in concrete, stone or metal, designed to fit into a structural
framework of masonry or wood.

SCULPTURE. The greatest contribution which art can make to garden
enrichment is complete, free-standing, three-dimensional sculpture. This is
more difficult and expensive to produce than any of the former types, and
therefore more rare. It is also more difficult to conceive and execute successfully. The standards of judgment for sculpture are fuzzier, less developed,
and more controversial than for the wall-fitting arts. The argument between
abstraction and representation is applied to sculpture, but it is less
convincing.

Sculpture of any size above perhaps 3 ft. becomes an independent element in the landscape. It may either compete or co-operate with structures or plant forms, depending upon how it is designed and placed. Ideally it is an integrated part of its setting in a garden or building, but this is a more complex connection than the decoration of a wall. The piece of sculpture must have a feeling of belonging where it is placed so completely that it would be a loss to remove it. This feeling has little to do with what subject the sculpture may appear to represent, or with how well it does represent it.

It is difficult to explain how this feeling of belonging can be produced. It usually takes a good professional sculptor to achieve it. Two paths can be followed: A piece of sculpture already created can have a site selected for it, and a setting designed around it to make it feel at home. Or a new piece of sculpture can be designed and executed for a specific site such as your garden might offer. Ideally, of course, a good landscape architect or architect, working with a good sculptor, could produce together complete ideas combining sculpture and setting in more refined ways than are commonly known.

Cost of Sculpture. The reader may very well object at this point that he thinks this all sounds just lovely, but very expensive, and how could he possibly afford it? This objection would be well taken. Custom-designed sculpture, or even good pieces already created, are far beyond the means of most of us. But this problem affects both sculptor and potential consumer. While the consumer starves for lack of sculpture (probably not knowing or believing he needs it), the sculptor starves for lack of customers and an audience. Serious efforts are being made by serious sculptors to produce pieces which can be duplicated, by casting or other means, enough to bring the cost down within ordinary reach. Parallel with these efforts other programs are being developed to prove to you, the consuming public, that sculpture can bring greater richness and interest into your home surroundings. For many of us the absence of purchasing power has caused any interest at all to die. This can be revived if we keep our minds open to the possibility.

Exorcising Prejudices. There are some who may say that, even if they could afford it, they would not buy sculpture anyway. It is too ostentatious, it looks funny, it makes them uncomfortable, what do they need it for, and so on. They have forgotten, or have never learned (through no fault of their own) that the function of the artist has always been to show us new ways of seeing, experiencing, and understanding the world about us. It has been said that if science is the art of knowing, art is the science of feeling. We may know all about the world, but we still cannot understand it without feeling about it as well. The absence of real art experience from the daily lives of most of us is one of the greatest weaknesses in our vaunted standard of

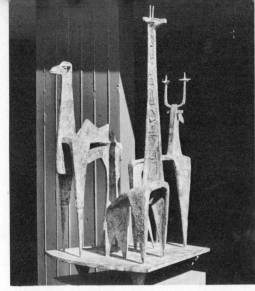

Sculpture by Bernard Rosenthal; photo by Julius Shulman

Sculpture by Claire Falkenstein; photo by Braun-Childress-Halberstadt

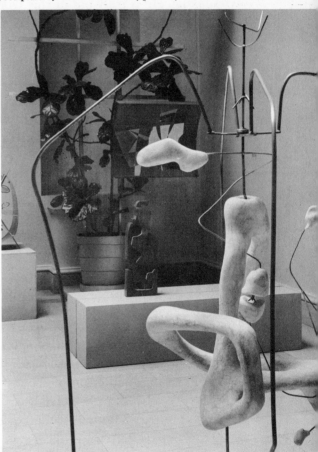

Sculpture by Bernard Rosenthal

living. The simplest African grows up surrounded by good music, painting, and sculpture which are integral parts of his daily life.

You and the Sculptor. You may well retort that neither the little boy holding the dolphin in the middle of the lily pool, nor that incomprehensible abstraction you saw at the museum last Sunday, are any help to you in understanding or appreciating your world. You may say that you would as soon have some nice rocks. And your complaint is justified. The little boy is a sentimental relic of the Renaissance, so worn out with copying and recasting that he has lost all meaning. The abstraction is produced by an artist who is lost without an audience, and therefore has left this world for one of his own making. He is truly out of this world. But the raw rocks have as yet no touch of human understanding. With your help the abstract artist could be brought back, and could give you very good service in improving your artistic standard of living. Although his work may seem crazy, he is highly skilled and knows a great deal about sculpture.

The process of bringing him back is relatively simple. He needs primarily a consistently interested audience, of adequate size, for a considerable period of time, and some help in earning a living. He can repay this simple aid very fully in service to his audience. This has been proved by all the experience of history.

SMALLER ART FORMS. There are other fields of art which are less controversial and more obviously useful in the garden. These include ceramics, glass, and any other types of craft or machine-produced art objects which will take the weather. Tank ends from boiler factories, up to 7 ft. in diameter, make very elegant large bowls for plants or water, if properly rustproofed.

The one important criterion of art objects for the garden is size. They must be larger than interior objects to be convincing out-of-doors. Two feet is perhaps a minimum dimension for any such object in the garden. This increases the production problems for materials such as ceramics, pottery, and glass, but they can be solved. Architectural Pottery is an outstanding example of such a solution. Ceramics are endlessly rich and wonderful in competent hands. Often in junk yards and stores one can find old bottles, dishes, or other objects, perhaps discarded as too large for the house, which would be just right in the garden.

We might end this discussion of art for the garden by pointing out that the entire process of putting together a garden, whether or not it has any art objects or even any structures in it, is an art process. Furthermore it cannot possibly succeed unless it is an art process, for successful gardens cannot be produced by purely practical standards alone.

Choice

The choice among all these diverse kinds of enrichment elements will be mostly personal, based on desire and need. The first pitfall is to get too many of them. They must be controlled, restricted, and organized along with the balance of the garden, or they are apt to disrupt and clutter it. The second pitfall, perhaps more seductive than the first, is to begin the accumulation of enrichment elements before the primary framework of surfacing, enclosure and shelter has been established. Many, many gardeners have made this mistake, usually unconsciously, with the result that the primary framework gets sidetracked, and often never materializes. The prettiest flower garden in the world falls flat without an adequate background and framing.

Enrichment elements take considerable time, money, and maintenance. Once started they are apt to consume all your resources. That is why they should be explored after the more basic elements. Although these enrichment elements include those most interesting to gardeners and others who appreciate the outdoors—in other words most garden consumers—they are nevertheless not the source of maximum interest and richness in the garden. This source is the over-all design, planning, or conception of three-dimensional form. If this is well done, the garden will be successful with either the barest essentials or the richest collection of elements. Without such over-all imagination no garden can succeed, no matter how much money and labor may be spent on it.

Architectural pottery

10. Plants and Planting

Many, many volumes of poetry and of poetic prose have been written about plants and planting. Some of this has been well written, some badly written; some beautiful, some corny. With the intentions of all these writers there can be no disagreement. Plants are endlessly fascinating: endlessly gracious; endlessly lovely; endlessly strong, persistent, and adaptable; magnificent and fragile; colorful and variable; rich in structure and form, color, and texture; architectural and sculptural and natural all at once; filled with potentiality for the free harmony of a beautiful world.

The larger plants live with us in the air space of the landscape, resisting and eluding gravity in the upward aspiration of their growth, yet firmly anchored, with their roots entrenched in the solid earth. Plants live in the air and in the earth at once. Each and every plant encloses a structure of marvelous articulation and delicacy, ranging in scale from the diminutive moss clump to the giant tropical banyan tree.

Every plant, even of the prostrate or clinging kinds, is a study in most delicate equilibrium, in a most harmonious adjustment of many parts to meet the needs of the whole. The root structure, spreading or deep below ground, balances in cubic volume the vegetative structure above ground. It anchors the plant in one place, and forms that firm yet flexible base from which the upper parts defy gravity and the vagaries and violences of the weather. From this firm clutch upon the bosom of mother earth the plant reaches toward light and air in balanced radial symmetry. Though often distorted by weather, site, or other plants, it is always in balance, always a display of the endless variety of biological construction, more delicate, elegant, flexible, sturdy, or massive than any structure man has yet produced..

Upon this lithe and tenacious structure, with its permanent or changing costuming in all the richness of foliage, are borne seasonally, intermittently, or constantly the flowers and fruit. That collection of delicately articulated jewels of unparalleled variety in form, color, and texture has been one of the chief delights and pursuits of gardeners since man first settled down on the land.

A plant is a living, growing structure, a unit of life. From the quick annual wild flower to the mighty redwoods and big trees which antedate the Christian church, every plant changes in form and aspect from day to day or from season to season. Plants are the bridge from inert matter to organic life, the spark plug in the great life-cycle of water, soil, plants, and animals. The process of photosynthesis carried on by the chlorophyll in the plants of this world is its basic production relation, basic to the growth of the landscape, basic to the animal kingdom, basic to the societies of man. Our ornamental planting—our shade trees and hedges and flowers, our cacti and succulents and alpines, our bog gardens and aquatics, our lawns and meadows—as it functions in forming and enriching the spaces in which we live, is at the same time symbolic to us of the wild life-cycle of primeval nature, and of the organized life-cycle of human agriculture.

Plant Science

Farmers and gardeners alike must understand plants in order to obtain the best results from growing them. Scientific or objective knowledge of plants is called botany. There are various branches of botanical science: (1) *morphology and physiology,* which are concerned with the structure and function of each individual plant body; (2) *ecology,* which is concerned first with the relations between each plant and the atmosphere and soil in which it lives, and second with the relations between different kinds of plants in groups or communities; (3) *taxonomy,* which is concerned with the identification and classification of all the different kinds of plants in the world; and (4) *horticulture,* which is concerned with the scientific development of plants for certain specific human uses and purposes. All of these are important to the development of your home grounds if plants are important to it. If you are bored with plants and with gardening, it is better not to use them than to use them badly. (You can solve your outdoor problems with structural elements.) If you are a green thumber who works by intuition, you are lucky that your intuition happens to follow the scientific paths.

Morphology and physiology are important because each plant is a living organism. These studies are basic to school and college botany courses.

William Aplin

Halberstadt

Paul J. Peart

Childress-Halberstadt

Paul J. Peart

Ecology is important because the health and quality of each plant depend upon what happens to it and around it during its lifetime. These external factors include temperature (maximum, optimum, and minimum); light (intensity, quality, and duration); carbon dioxide concentration in the atmosphere; atmospheric humidity, precipitation, and wind movement; available water in the soil; soil temperature; amount of air in the soil; quantity and kinds of inorganic salts in solution in the soil; competition from other plants; pollinating insects for flowers and fruit; animal activity, such as grazing; the activity of beneficent soil bacteria and fungi; parasitic or destructive bacteria, fungi and insects; the presence of growth substances—hormones and vitamins, both natural and synthetic. In order to grow healthy and good-looking plants in your garden you have to know something about the requirements of each kind of plant in each of these factors.

Consideration of competition between plants leads to a very interesting section of ecology which deals with how and why plants live together in nature in certain typical groupings. As we have seen, different types of climate produce different types of natural vegetation—forest in the East and Northwest, grassland in the Midwest and Pacific Coast, shrubland (sagebrush, chaparral, desert brush) in the West. We modify this native vegetation in our gardens by establishing structural control or special horticultural practices (gardening). As soon as we relax these, our gardens tend to revert to the natural vegetation.

A knowledge of the processes which produce this natural vegetation will help us to think through our problems in planting design. Authorities such as Weaver and Clements describe these processes thoroughly.

Taxonomy. There are some 300,000 different kinds of plants in the world, and several thousand new kinds are discovered each year. In order to be able to identify and name each of these, botanists have developed a system of natural classification which enables each specific kind of plant to be known by the same name around the world. Although common names may be more familiar and easier to remember, they are not reliable. One plant may have several different common names in different regions, and there are many kinds of plants which have never become so commonly known as to acquire common names. For these reasons the botanical name is the only accurate way to identify a plant.

The botanical name consists of two words, usually Latinized. The first word, always capitalized, is the genus name; the second, not capitalized, is the species name. The species is the smallest unit of classification for plants. It includes all those that are essentially alike when grown under similar conditions, that interbreed freely, and that are more or less distinct from other kinds with which they do not interbreed freely.

Horticulture. According to Gardner, horticulture means garden culture, or the culture of garden crops and plants, and this implies cultivation within rather restricted areas. No one, however, has been able to say just how restricted the area must be to be called a *garden,* or how extensive it must be to be called a *field.*

In order to plant our gardens intelligently and successfully, we must have a fair understanding of certain fundamentals. Plants are living organisms which take in water and nutrients from the soil and carbon dioxide from the air, manufacture food in the foliage, and give off water and oxygen. Therefore they have a very delicate and sensitive relationship with the immediate local climate and soil in which they find themselves. They also have a delicate relationship with the other plants around them. In nature, plants of similar cultural requirements tend to group themselves together in communities in which the various species help each other to their best development. This principle is also of basic importance to any human planting scheme.

The science of horticulture can produce from wild plants improved domestic varieties which can scarely be recognized as still the same species. In addition to its contributions to all the crops which are basic to our standard of living, horticulture has made possible all the refined types of ornamental planting which we have available. There is no end to the possibilities of this refinement; new varieties, new combinations, new cultural procedures, and new ornamental plant communities are being explored and produced every day. Basic to this production process is a sympathetic relation between horticulture and landscape architecture.

Plant Selection

For the amateur gardener and garden designer, who has not the time or energy to go into scientific detail, all sorts of simplified handbooks and garden calendars have been developed to help him select plant materials.

HORTICULTURAL CLASSIFICATION FOR LANDSCAPING. Basic to such simplification is a rational classification of plant material for landscape use, in terms which help solve landscape problems. Botanical classification is essential to the identification of the material, but beyond that it is of little or no help in determining landscape uses. Horticultural or ecological classification is basic to landscape use, and we must refer to it constantly. Plants must be classified accurately in terms of their culture requirements somewhat as follows:

Temperature requirements or tolerances
    Minimum, maximum, and duration of each
    Optimum
Water requirements or tolerances
    Drought tolerance or moisture preference
    Sharp or slow subsurface drainage
    Atmospheric humidity
Light requirements or tolerances
    Full shade
    Filtered light
    Half-day sun and half-day shade (morning or afternoon)
    Full sun
Soil requirements or tolerances
    Rich or deep soil
    Sterile or shallow soil
    Sandy or rocky soil
    Clayey or adobe soil
    Acid soil
    Alkali soil
    Special feeding
Other characteristics
    Wind tolerance
    Special requirements for flowering and fruiting
    Training and pruning requirements
    Propagation methods
    Susceptibility to pests
    Susceptibility to diseases
    Tendency to become weedy in wrong location

These cultural classifications are suggestive; there are many more that can be added to the list. We need information on these points about each kind of plant we may want to use, and we need lists of plants suitable when each type of condition is encountered. We must remember that these factors affect each other. Plants make the best use of water and nutrients at optimum temperatures. They will endure lower temperatures if "hardened off" by reducing the application of water in the fall so that they contain no soft green growth. They will endure higher temperatures if properly and specially irrigated and if growing in specially prepared soil. Shade and sun requirements depend upon the locality; roses which require full sun near the seacoast will do well in the shade in the desert. Plants are less susceptible to pests and diseases if they are healthy and vigorous. And so on.

PHYSICAL CLASSIFICATION FOR LANDSCAPING. Horticultural classifications are the beginning but not the end of planting design. We must have a further and more specific system of classification for landscape uses. This has to be based on the actual physical character and properties of the plant, rather than any sort of botanical, naturalistic, sentimental, or literary associations, or upon personal prejudices, likes, and dislikes. Any of these latter elements may enter into the picture for you personally, but they should enter only after the rational physical facts have been analyzed and understood.

We select plants for our gardens to carry out certain desired arrangements which have been developed in plan, and to suit certain maintenance desires or possibilities which have been programmed. Thus the objective physical factors basic to the selection of plants for landscape use (and also to their classification for such use) are as follows:

1. The plan (desired arrangement) for surfacing, enclosure, shelter, enrichment
2. Cultural requirements (maintenance) as outlined
3. Ultimate size, rate of growth, and length of life
4. Natural form—silhouette and structure
5. Texture—size, form, and arrangement of foliage and structural members
6. Color—foliage, bark, stems, flowers, fruit
7. Fragrance.

ULTIMATE SIZE. Size involves height, spread, perhaps trunk diameter; how long the plant takes to reach such dimensions; whether they are attainable at all under a particular set of growing conditions; whether the plant grows so fast as to startle us, fast enough to give a feeling of reasonable progress, or so slowly as to become exasperating unless proper allowance has been made for it; and whether the plant should be considered permanent or temporary in the garden scheme. In terms of pure height we tend to sort out certain typical categories: ground covers up to 18 in. in height, low shrubs to 3 ft., medium shrubs to 6 ft., large shrubs to 10 ft., tall shrubs or small trees to 20 ft., medium trees to 50 ft., tall trees over 50 ft., moderate vines to 10 ft., tall vines over that. The maximum dimension is most important. For most plants it is vertical, but for many it is horizontal, or both.

Spacing: Plants are, in general, a series of units circular in plan, varying in diameter or spread from a few inches to 100 ft. or more, and in height from 1 or 2 in. to 200 ft., or more. With due regard to the selection factors listed, these units are independent of each other for arrangement purposes. They can be spaced so closely as to grow together, forming ground cover, hedges or shrub masses, or groves of trees. Or they can be spaced so far apart as

Morley Baer (2)

Morley Baer

Los Angeles Chamber of Commerce

Paul J. Peart

Paul J. Peart

never to be able to touch, so that each plant can develop into a perfect speci-men (as in an orchard). These different spacings will affect the form of the plants; they will take different forms when crowded than when standing free. Spacing also affects the time it takes to produce a mature or well developed quality.

The primary reason for placing ultimate size third in our list of selection factors is that plants should always be spaced so that they can continue to grow and develop in the forms and arrangements planned. If after two years, you unexpectedly find it necessary to trim the shrubs regularly, something was wrong with the original selection or arrangement. We tend to crowd slow plants more than those which grow faster, but eventually the same problems of trimming or thinning will develop. Even planting planned for pruning or trimming, like espaliers or hedges, must take into account size and growth habits in order to succeed.

Rate of Growth: The relation between ultimate size and rate of growth emphasizes the distinctive character of plants as living and obviously chang-ing material. The rate of change and development of most plants, and their flexibility in adjusting to their habitat, make it necessary to project and visualize three-dimensional arrangements ahead in time 6 months, 5 years or 50 years. With annual flowers you can project ahead one season's effects, but with major shrubs and trees you will want to plan an arrangement which will develop and accumulate character and maturity year after year. There-fore any particular species of shrub or tree should be guaranteed occupancy of its portion of the site long enough to develop reasonably mature character. This means that the use of the land should be planned ahead as far as pos-sible, in order to avoid major rearrangements.

Full-grown Material: The complexity of visualizing the maturity of the planting scheme 5 to 50 years ahead can, of course, be offset by the use of oversize or full-grown material. Up-to-date nurserymen and big tree special-ists have developed great ingenuity and skill in handling large plants. How-ever, the cost of such specimens is apt to be beyond the average budget, except perhaps for a tree or two in just the most important spots. As we go up in nursery size we find a limitation on our choice of kinds. Many cannot be handled easily in large sizes, and nurseries can seldom afford to maintain large stocks of specimen material. This latter problem, of course, does not exist in the more humid parts of the country where collecting from nature is common practice. There is also a good deal to be said for the experience of planting small in order to watch the plants grow and adjust to their planned arrangement. Plants put in in small sizes are very apt to outgrow larger sizes in a few years, because they become established more easily, and have not had the shocks and restrictions of nursery handling. This rule does not hold for material which is slow-growing, or slow to establish itself. It must be said, however, that nothing will stabilize and solidify a newly planted garden like the moving in of a mature tree or specimen plant.

NATURAL FORM. The form of any growing plant is a result of the combination of two factors. One is the typical form it tends to develop as a result of its heredity. The other is the modifications or distortions it may develop as a result of its specific environment. To speak of natural form is incomplete; we must ask: Natural form where? Under what conditions? The single pine in the open meadow, the pine crowded with many others in a dense grove and the pine on exposed mountain top or seashore will scarcely be recognizable as belonging to the same species. In planting design we must do three things:

1. Visualize a certain kind of form
2. Select kinds which tend to develop in that direction
3. Create conditions which will encourage such development.

As we go further into the detail of plant forms, their richness in variety expands rapidly. The variations in ultimate dimensions, in height and spread and rate of growth, become simplicity itself when we consider the fantastic variability in general form and structure within the ornamental plant world. With the circular plan form of the single unit as a common denominator, we have a range of form in elevation from those which are horizontal in the proportion of as much as 1 unit of height to 10 or 12 of spread, through every imaginable intermediate variation to those which are vertical in the proportion of 10:1, height to spread. Structural forms go through all variations of symmetry and irregularity. From horizontal to vertical, from regular to irregular, from symmetrical to contorted, from rigid to pliable, from erect to prostrate, from climbing to crawling, from the open tracery to the dense mass, the variation is endless. In relation of outline silhouette to supporting structure, and in relation of these to size and rate of growth, the variability becomes more and more complex.

We can list among trees the round-headed, the spreading, the irregular, the vertical oval, the slender upright, the weeper, the fastigiate, the vertical with horizontal branches, and so on. But their further breakdown into all the angular and curving, regular and irregular, opposite and alternate relations of twig to branch to trunk presents a difficult problem of classification.

Most trees take one form when they are young, another as they mature, and a third as they grow old. Shrubs, too, change character with maturity. Especially the larger and more erect species tend to open up and lose their lower branches, becoming semi-tree forms. This tendency is subject to control or promotion by pruning. These woody lower structures have considerable character and interest. They can become assets in the garden, rather than liabilities which have to be concealed.

Plants whose horizontal dimensions tend to exceed their vertical dimensions are most useful as ground covers. Conversely, plants whose vertical dimensions tend to exceed their horizontal are more useful for the enclosure of garden space at the sides, for boundary and division planting. There are, of course, certain radial clump forms which fall between and can be used for either. Enclosure plants below eye level mark boundaries and divisions of space and make patterns in the garden. Above eye level they tend to become screens of varying thickness and density.

TEXTURE. From variations in structure and silhouette to variations in texture is a step from complexity to infinity. It is from this relation between foliage and structure that most of us recognize and identify plants as they are generally used in landscape design. This is particularly true of the larger material, the woody and semi-woody shrubs and trees, the sizeable herbaceous material, the climbers, trailers, and sprawlers.

In size foliage ranges from the tiny scales of heather and juniper, through all the intermediate variations of "ordinary" garden plants, to the startling extremes of *Magnolia triflora,* palms, elephant ears, bananas, and philodendron.

In form, foliage is classified in a range typified by linear (pine needles), lanceolate (lance-shaped), ovate (oval), obovate (fat oval), cordate (heart-shaped), and so on. Complicating these are intermediates (linear-lanceolate, cordate-obovate); variations from symmetry in the individual leaf; variations in the edge (simple, toothed, holly-like, lobed) and in the point; special forms; variations in thickness and stiffness, and varying combinations of these (thick-soft, thin-stiff); variations in veining; variations in pinnation, (dissection of the leaf into a few or many smaller leaflets); variations in the texture of each leaf (smooth-glossy, smooth-dull, fuzzy, crinkled, etc.); variations in the length and angle of the petiole connecting leaf to twig or stem; and so on. The variation in foliage, like the variation in rocks, is endless and endlessly fascinating.

In foliage arrangement on the plant structure, we have further wide variation: from thin-scattered to dense-crowded, from even-all-over-the-plant to grouped-in-bunches-or-tufts, from erect through horizontal to pendant, from stiff to pliable to tremulous, from sprinkles through fronds to clumps, the range can scarcely be cataloged. Consider these in relation to variations in leaf form, leaf size, plant structure and silhouette, size and rate of growth, as well as color, and the limitless richness of the plant palette becomes increasingly obvious.

A further important variation in the textural quality of plants appears in those which are deciduous, that is, which develop a permanent woody structure but lose their leaves in winter. The great virtue, richness, and interest of deciduous plants lies precisely in those continuous seasonal changes which are associated in so many minds with the cold and storms of Eastern winters. From the fresh light greens and bronzes of bursting spring through the rich mature greens of summer and the gorgeous reds, browns, and yellows of fall to the complete and elegant exposure of trunk, branch, and stem structure during the winter we can enjoy a continuous show unmatched for variety and interest.

COLOR. Color makes the world comprehensible, vibrant, and magnificent for us. In its purer and stronger forms it comes best in fractional quantities, save for special or seasonal bursts, within a general framework of greens, browns, and blues. Each of these is generally grayed with some admixture of the other and with changes in light and atmosphere relations. The purer and stronger the color we introduce, the more carefully considered must be its quantity, and its relations with other colors and elements around it. It is important to use color in a disciplined and controlled fashion which will strengthen, rather than disrupt, the general form and pattern of garden and street. This does not necessarily eliminate the "riot of color." It merely sets it in a frame which holds it down and eliminates fatigue in the spectator.

Color in plants is normally thought of as flower or fruit color, because those are the most striking. But foliage and structure likewise have color of considerable range. In foliage this runs from gray, blue-gray, and brown-gray through gray-green, light, medium and dark green, to various purple and red shades, not to mention variegations of silver, yellow, and red. In bark it runs from birch white through many grays and browns to the shiny reds of madrone, manzanita, and river birch, and some near-blacks. These colors are usually grayed and toned down by contrast with the clarity of flower and fruit colors. They are also subject to considerable variation under different conditions of soil, atmosphere, cultivation, climate, and season.

Foliage Patterns. There is a climate zone pattern of these colors, particularly in foliage. The strong clear greens and variegations seem to be produced by the more humid zones, the tropical and temperate forests. As we move into the more arid zones, both hot and cold, the foliage colors in native trees and shrubs tend toward grays, gray-greens, brown-greens, and the general landscape quality becomes thinner, paler, browner, or grayer. Likewise textures seem to vary by zones: the fine glossy surfaces develop in the more humid zones, the dull and fuzzy ones in the drier zones where they act as protective coverings.

However, we people have a tendency to equalize environments in order to make them more liveable. We plant trees in hot dry sections to cool them off, though none grew there before. In cold wet country we cut down the trees to let in the sun. In the more humid zones, particularly where it becomes uncomfortable (as in the tropics), or where coolness and fog prevail (as our northwest coast), the darker, heavier, glossier greens tend to accentuate the oppressive or discomforting qualities of the atmosphere. Here we are apt to encourage the lighter, clearer greens; to use thinner forms in cool zones; and even silver and gold variegations in zones where the atmosphere is dull and dark. In the arid zones, on the other hand, where light, heat, and dryness press upon us, we tend to promote the growth of dark, bright, glossy, or clear greens, the larger and richer foliage which feels cool and moist. This we do by artificially increasing the humidity—that is, by irrigation. We seek two values in every landscape:

1. The expression of its native quality
2. The development of maximum human livability.

These values need not be incompatible.

Flowers and Fruit: Flowers and fruit must be considered in two relations: on the plant which bears them, and cut and arranged in containers in the house. Growing flowers should be separated according to whether they are primarily to be seen in the garden or to be cut for house use. The latter are difficult, though not impossible to use in the garden scheme. Maintenance procedures are apt to be simplified if they are grown in functional rows in the workspace or service yard.

If we are concerned primarily with flowers and fruit on plants in the garden, we must also be concerned with the size and form of those plants. The first distinction is between the woody plants and the herbaceous material. The latter include the general run of garden annuals and perennials, bulbs, alpines, bog plants, aquatics, succulents, annual and perennial vines, and so on. This herbaceous material is in general smaller—below eye level—more seasonal, and less permanent than the woody material. Therefore it is displayed best within a more permanent framework and background of shrubs and trees or structural elements. In such a setting the great loveliness and interest of this type of material can be brought out so as to delight the gardener's heart.

Woody Plants: Those of us who are not gardeners are apt to avoid the cultural complications of herbaceous plantings, except perhaps for a few hardy reliables such as hollyhocks or naturalized bulbs. Instead we search for color in the permanent woody plants which are the main framework of the garden. They do produce showy color: from the spring blossoms and fall foliage of the Northeast, through the camellias, rhododendrons, and berried pyracantha-cotoneaster of the West Coast, the magnolia and crepe myrtle of the Deep South, to the hibiscus, oleander and trumpet vines of the semiarid Southwest. However, as plants get larger and more permanent they must be selected more carefully for specific situations. We can plant anything we want to experiment with in our seasonal borders without great loss in time or money. There we can play with pure color to our heart's content. But with 5-year shrubs and 20-year trees we must be more judicious; we must consider not only the color they can produce for us, but the full size, the rate of growth, the form and structure, the texture, whether deciduous or evergreen, and so on. The tree which is good for summer shade and winter sun, the shrub which will give us enclosure and privacy, may not also be the kind to produce flowers or fruit for us. Those trees and shrubs which do give us all these things are the ones we tend to choose more and more often.

Color Ranges. On the limitless fascination in form and color of flowers and fruit, both ornamental and edible, we need hardly elaborate. Better poets than we have given us lyric and delicately subtle descriptions. The great horticulturists and gardeners of our times have concentrated their energies on the production of constantly improved varieties, more double flowers, larger, brighter, and clearer. If we were to raise a still small voice it might only be to wonder if sometimes the flower doesn't run away with the plant, as in the proliferation of hybrid tea roses. But that is a matter of a general climate of opinion.

The colors of flowers and fruits, especially the herbaceous material, run the gamut. The complex delights of planning the perennial border for all seasons and all color relations have been explored for us in endless garden books and manuals. True blues, especially in deeper and stronger shades, are the choicest and scarcest colors in flower and fruit. Otherwise the general range, through red, pink, yellow, orange, lavender, purple, and white, with all imaginable intermediate variations, is well known and often described. The subtle variations—such as pure pink which is merely pale red, carmine pink which has blue in it, salmon pink which has yellow in it—are subject to subtle and delicate handling even as the oils and water colors of the painter's palette.

While we occasionally see color combinations which make us somewhat seasick, we are inclined to be skeptical of ready-made systems. We think stronger and more contrasting color combinations than those normally considered "good taste" may be perfectly good and reasonable, with proper proportions and framing. Such combinations are somewhat like food: it's a question of what you have been educated to and are used to. Generally those colors having some content of the general landscape colors—brown, green, blue—are best in exposed quantities. Those of more primary or synthetic quality should be held to smaller quantities and more specially planned locations and relations to other colors.

FRAGRANCE. One further factor relevant to the selection of plants is that of fragrance or odor. It is produced mainly by flowers, but also by damaged fruit or vegetative parts in many plants. It may be pleasant or unpleasant; naturally we try to avoid the latter. Careful fragrance relations are another delicate refinement of the planting scheme, tending to be quite vulnerable to subjective personal reactions. Thus some may prefer strong fragrance, some mild fragrance, some none. Such touches as the use of rosemary and myrtle along paths and steps, where brushing them releases the aroma of the foliage, are very pleasant and seldom controversial.

Unity and Variety

The object of planting is not only to work into the garden scheme all the different kinds of plants which you would like to have for one reason or another. It is also to put them together in a continuous framework or pattern which will unify the garden space somewhat as the structure of the house unifies the space inside it, although more loosely. The variety of plants which are offered for use in our gardens may often seem complex and confusing. But it is the analysis and classification of this variety in terms of size, form, texture, and color which suggest to us various ways to achieve unity without losing interest. We can have unity by size: one or a few kinds of larger trees and shrubs can dominate and unify many more kinds of smaller plants. Variety increases as we go down the size scale; decreases as we go up. Or we can have unity by form: strong forms, as the columnar or the weeping, may establish a dominant framework for a variety of looser forms. We can have unity by texture: the large-dark-glossy or the thin-light-fine may predominate throughout one size of plants, or through several sizes. Likewise we can have unity by color repetition, in foliage or structure or flowers or fruit. While the actual know-how for arranging such unified patterns may seem to be a professional monopoly; anyone willing to study and analyze can arrive at some portion of it.

The patterns of unity must be related to eye-level patterns. There is a ground-cover pattern, of grass, herbaceous materials, and low woody planting. There is an eye-level pattern of tall herbs and grasses, medium and tall shrubs, and small trees. And there is an overhead pattern of tree structure and foliage. These patterns can be unified within or among themselves.

NATIVE OR FOREIGN PLANTS. The relation between native or indigenous and foreign or exotic plants has been a source of controversy in landscape circles for many years. The two extremes in this controversy can be represented approximately as follows: "A" rejects all local or regional wild plants as "weeds," common, vulgar, coarse, and so on; clears the land (perhaps a hangover from colonial days); and brings in refined garden species without reference to their original homeland. "B," on the other hand, rises in righteous indignation to the defense of the beauties of the local landscape and vegetation; condemns foreign introductions as disruptive of the local loveliness—inappropriate, blatant, gaudy, gauche, and so on, and as sickly exotics which will never be really healthy no matter how carefully pampered; whereas the lusty natives will grow and thrive with little or no care. Both sides have points worth making.

The range of plants useful to general landscape design extends from those surviving with reasonable health the normal local garden conditions through those surviving the local wild conditions. This entire range usually will include plants of both local and foreign origin. In the humid to subhumid East there is less difference between garden and wild conditions than in the arid to semiarid West, where all gardening depends upon irrigation. Therefore in the East there need be little noticeable boundary between garden areas and wild or natural areas (if your lot is big enough to include them) while in the West there is bound to be a noticeable boundary between irrigated and unirrigated areas. Thus in Eastern gardens local and imported plants can mingle more freely than in the West, where few natives can adapt themselves to the constant watering of average garden culture. In the East the enforcing of a choice between natives and exotics as such may be more subjective than in the West, where it has a horticultural basis. However, even in the West exotics from similar climates will naturalize in the wild, and some natives will adjust to garden conditions.

SELECTION. Our problem is always to select the plant which will grow best while doing what we want it to do in a specific planned location. This is the right plant in the right place—the gardener's ideal. Selection is based on the best analysis of soil and climate in that spot location, and the best prediction for the future continuity of those conditions. Such selections should be made from the broadest possible list of available material, at least until local practice boils down to some few specific plants which are sure to do the best job in such specific locations. (Usually local practice is partly accidental and partly rational. Its habitual materials for hedges, ground covers, or trees are not necessarily the best possible choices.) Restriction of the choice list—to natives only, exotics only, or any other arbitrary "only"—

is apt to eliminate the most relevant plant for a particular spot. The original nativity of the plants on the list is only relevant insofar as it may give us a clue to their adaptability to local conditions.

Selection, arrangement, and maintenance form the basic triangle of planting design. We select plants to develop a desired plan arrangement which will not exceed a certain desirable maintenance load. Or we plan an arrangement to include certain desired plants previously selected, and we are prepared to provide the maintenance they require in order to have them. Or, again, we determine whether we prefer maximum or minimum maintenance, or something in between, and then select plants and plan an arrangement which will produce that for us.

Arrangement

The arrangement of plants in and on the ground is a rich and fascinating art. It has its own laws and disciplines, based on full analysis of the material. Once these are understood they become a gateway to freedom of design comparable to painting or sculpture.

Plants don't have to hold each other up. The relations established between these plant units, the ground, and structural elements depend entirely upon the designer. The plants can be spaced so far apart as never to touch, always to remain detached circles. Or they can be so crowded as to form continuous mats on the ground (lawns), masses above ground (screens), or canopies overhead (woods). They can be spaced regularly and geometrically, or completely irregularly, or in any variation or combination between. Combinations of definite geometric plan skeletons with irregular clumps and groupings are both possible and desirable. Anything goes in plant grouping and arrangement if the people who are to see it like it, if it will grow well, and if the maintenance required is not excessive.

Arrangements of planting on most sites will proceed through the basic stages of surfacing, enclosure, shelter, and enrichment, as discussed in chapters 6–9. These are the most practical stages, in terms of erosion control, screening, shade, and color. They are also the most esthetic stages in terms of the development of rich site-space form through the structural yet spatial use of plant material. In other words, we don't solve the practical problems first and then beautify them; we develop beautiful solutions for the practical problems in their broadest definition, which includes the human values needed in the landscape.

Maintenance

Maintenance is gardening, horticulture by yourself with or without hired help in your own back and front yards. It is cutting the grass and trimming the shrubs, pulling weeds and spraying bugs, pruning and feeding and sprinkling or irrigating. Some of us enjoy gardening and some of us don't. Until recently gardens were designed and handbooks written for those who liked it, or would hire good gardeners to do it for them. The rest were left in a no-man's-land of uncut lawns, untrimmed shrubs, and unpulled weeds.

MINIMUM REQUIREMENTS.   A few years ago some landscape architects began to think about designing for minimum maintenance. Now it is possible to think about gardens for gardeners and gardens for nongardeners, and any combination in between. However, it must be said that in the planted garden there still has to be a certain minimum amount of maintenance. The only garden which has no gardening activity at all is that which is all paving, walls, and structural shelter, or that which is left completely to nature. The structural garden ("with a lawn of green concrete") is perfectly possible and functional at the scale of the average yard, with some additional outlay of cash and labor at the beginning. The garden which is left to nature is an intriguing and romantic theory which seldom works out completely in practice, except in very special situations.

Modifying Natural Succession: The processes of ecology in untouched nature produce balanced plant communities which are self-maintaining as long as they are undisturbed. As soon as we disturb the natural ecological communities—as we must in order to develop farms or build homes or communities of our own—we start the succession over again, beginning with the first ragged weedy invaders. If left alone after the initial disturbance, our land will sooner or later go back to the typical local wild vegetation.

The problem of gardening begins with our desire to change the proportions, character, or material of that vegetation. We usually want a more balanced relation between trees, shrubs, and grass than nature is apt to produce for us on our lot. Furthermore, we tend to equalize climatic extremes and bring them toward a golden mean. Thus in forest areas we open up larger grass areas to let in the sun. In grass areas we plant trees for shade and shrubs for enclosure and windbreak. In dry brushland we introduce irrigated trees and grass areas for shade and coolness.

Beyond changing the proportions of the basic types of vegetation we embark upon any or all of the intriguing multitude of horticultural practices. If we want to introduce kinds of trees or shrubs which are not indigenous, we become involved in the cultural analysis we have discussed. The mown grass lawn is a humanized refinement of the wild meadow, dependent entirely upon maintenance for its quality. The development of the incidental herbaceous colonies of natural communities into the complex delights of continuous perennial, annual, and bulb borders is a long and arduous, though highly rewarding, process.

Thus in our gardens we can go back to nature if we are really prepared to let her have her way. We can go to garden architecture to establish immediate, precise, and more permanent control of our outdoor living space. We can dabble in horticulture, with the possibility of becoming more and more interested in it (if we are not already). Or we can combine all three approaches in varying proportions. This last is what usually happens, through the accidents and expedients of the search for practical solutions within one's resources. This combined approach is also the most productive and has the greatest potential for rich, beautiful, and livable gardens. In order to get the most out of it it is well to understand the nature of its component parts—nature, structure, and horticulture—as outlined above.

ANTICIPATION OF MAINTENANCE. The most sensitive selection, the most imaginative arrangement, are useless without adequate careful maintenance follow-through. The key to the success of any planting program is the closeness of its integration with the maintenance program which must carry it on to full development. This program must expand as the local soil and climate become less favorable to the kind of development desired. Certainly if maintenance is not a guaranteed part of a landscape program we must go to some sort of permanent structural control of surface and enclosure, or to the limited range of plants which can be depended upon to perform without maintenance. Cultural considerations are the beginning, not the end, of planting design; but first things must come first. Selection and arrangement must be synchronized with maintenance through a determination of the amount that will be available, followed by a careful check to see that the plans do not demand more than this amount. Determination of the areas to be left in the hands of nature, those to be controlled by structural surfacing and enclosure, and those to be developed with planting which will require care, must be done with an eye to this factor.

There is, of course, wide latitude in the amounts of maintenance inherent in planting design. A great many of the ordinary kinds of planting development force the performance of thoroughly unnecessary amounts. Too little attention has been paid to the design of planting for minimum maintenance, especially in relation to maximum effect. Plants should be selected which will grow well in the given location without more care than can be provided,

Roger Sturtevant

Dean Stone

Dean Stone

Dean Stone

and which will have room to grow to their full ultimate size without persistent laborious trimming. In general, a careful analysis of the nature and amount of maintenance operations required for various kinds of planting should be made, and this analysis should become a part of design thinking.

REDUCING MAINTENANCE.   Garden elements requiring most maintenance work are:

1. Lawn, particularly in its more refined and pure forms, and in complex shapes with edges difficult to trim.
2. Annual and perennial flowers.
3. Trimmed hedges.
4. Trimmed shrubs and trees.
5. Plants requiring special soil, continuous watering or continuous spraying for pests.

Thus, in order to reduce garden work try these suggestions:

Lawn. In small spaces use grass only where you want to walk or sit on it. If the walking or sitting is to be heavy, substitute paving. In other areas substitute ground covers, such as ivy, periwinkle, or low spreading shrubs. Install mowing edges between lawn and flower or shrub beds. Think of the operation of a mower when laying out your lawn forms, and when placing obstacles, such as trees or specimen shrubs, in the grass.

In areas large enough for power mowing, grass is still the most practical and pleasant surface. At that scale detail of mix is less important, intruders can naturalize, edges can be rough, mowing keeps both weeds and grass down, water and fertilizer keep the grass healthy.

Annual and Perennial Flowers. For color and enrichment, concentrate on relatively permanent perennials—such as geraniums or daylilies—or colorful shrubs and trees, or structural elements like sculpture, murals, or rocks. If you want to grow flowers, vegetables, or herbs, plant them in raised beds which eliminate stooping, protect the plants, and make an attractive pattern all year.

Trimmed Hedges, Shrubs, and Trees. Study plant growth to avoid laborious and deforming trimming by selecting kinds whose ultimate natural size and shape will be most nearly correct. Most woody plants, however, require occasional careful and intelligent pruning. Remember that fences and walls provide more screening with less trouble than shrubs. Also remember that for a given function—shade trees, boundary screen, interior division—it requires less maintenance to use fewer kinds of plants. This does not mean that the shorter the plant list the better the garden—it only means somewhat less work with such problems as installation and replacement.

Plants Requiring Special Care. Skip these unless you want to care for them.

Also, plan a garden work center so equipment is handily stored, easy to find, and in good condition. Provide ramps and openings for wheeled tools and equipment.

Good practice in watering and weeding, cultivating and fertilizing, pruning and spraying, seeding, planting and transplanting, and all the other rational technical aspects of gardening and horticulture vary from region to region and locale to locale. Much excellent reference material, many lectures, study groups, schools, and organizations are at hand to advise, help, and guide the neophyte in the garden. We need not try to duplicate their efforts in detail here, but we must stress the dependence of most planting design upon good maintenance. This does not necessarily mean a continuous horticultural program. It does mean that the maintenance program has to be a part of the design of the garden, whether simple or elaborate, and that its continuity must be guaranteed. It is useless, for instance, to plan a large lawn unless someone is sure to mow, feed, and water it; or to plan a long flower border unless someone is prepared to grow and rotate the annuals, divide the perennials, lift, store, and replant the bulbs, and so on. Even standard trees and shrubs need certain basic attention to their supply of food and water down where the roots are.

NATURAL FACTORS IN MAINTENANCE. The maintenance aspects of gardening are fundamentally simple in principle. They are concerned primarily with five factors which affect the growth of plants: temperature, water, light, nutrients, and pests. These all act in combination rather than singly.

OTHER FACTORS. There are, of course, other factors important in gardening, especially as one's interests become more specialized. These include training and pruning, breeding, propagation, hormones and other growth regulators, and the culture of special kinds or groups of plants. We must emphasize that these paragraphs are no more than a sketchy outline of certain aspects of horticultural factors and problems as they have been impressed upon us in the actual practice of designing and building gardens. A complete handbook or textbook—such as Gardner's BASIC HORTICULTURE— is essential to complete understanding of the subject. Good regional handbooks are also invaluable.

Garden maintenance is neither good nor bad as an activity, except as it affects you personally. We can design gardens for maximum maintenance and horticultural activity, or for minimum maintenance. Each extreme can be of equal esthetic quality and human livability. Another way to express

this is in terms of neatness in the garden. We have wide ranges in attitude toward this: from the enthusiastic gardener who never lets a weed get past seed leaves, a dead leaf or twig lie on grass or terrace, or a dead flower remain in the border, to the disinterested one who never cuts the grass, prunes the shrubs, or pulls a weed. Desirable practice for most of us will obviously lie between these extremes. We must remember that nature, once ecological balance is established, is very neat. This is true even though the ground may be covered with leaves and with seedlings popping up through them. These are all part of basic natural processes, and one reason for having a garden is to put ourselves in touch with such processes. Perhaps the point at which each of us should stop worrying about neatness is that at which we feel the garden becomes our master instead of our servant.

The one maintenance activity which is artistic as well as scientific is pruning. This requires sympathetic understanding of the material, whereas trimming requires merely the tools. The ultimate form development of a plant, other things being equal, is entirely dependent upon the kind of pruning it needs and receives. There are plants which will develop a mature specimen character with no pruning whatsoever, and there are those which will take no form at all without constant vigorous pruning. Most plants lie between these extremes. The pruner should approach his material with all the care and circumspection exercised by a sculptor in approaching a block of stone. Both are concerned with the removal of portions of the material to produce a more perfect form. Pruning is an art requiring a great deal of thought and sound judgment. Each plant has to be studied as an individual, have its esthetic possibilities analyzed, and then be given that treatment which will best further those possibilities. The practice of "trimming the shrubs" is only the lazy way to avoid taking this problem seriously.

11. Procedure

How does one go about all this planning and design of public access, general living, work spaces, and private living; of surfacing and enclosure and shelter and enrichment; of selection, arrangement, and maintenance?

First, you must have a site and a program. Either of these may come first, depending upon your particular problem. The site is the lot, the real estate, the piece of land with or without a house already on it, on which you intend to carry out some sort of development. This site is a piece of land which is soil having certain physical properties, with air-space above it and some sort of landscape—urban, suburban, rural, or natural—around it. It may also have on it various sorts of buildings, trees or other plants, rocks, water, or miscellaneous features. All of these must be studied for possible use or disuse.

The program, in writing, lists all your needs, desires, resources, and limitations—physical things you want or don't want, psychological effects you want or don't want, and so on. Ideally, you will write a complete program for a complete home unit including both house and garden; then you will look for a site to suit these purposes. However, the program must be written sooner or later. If you already have a site, even if you already have a house on it, you should still begin your new thinking by writing a program.

The Plan

Second, you must have a plan—you must design your new landscape. This means drawing accurately on paper the actual detailed form projected for the new development. We do this because it makes possible complete thinking which is more imaginative as well as more practical. It is easier to plan in advance than to try to figure out the forms and arrangements on the job as you go along, and they come out better. It makes it possible to foresee all sorts of complications which may arise to stop the job if you haven't planned for them. It prevents spending money on materials and labor without being sure of the results. It lets you know where you are going before you begin. This is just as exciting and adventurous as plunging in without a plan. Your journey is much more interesting with one.

SCALE. Drawing a plan to scale is a technique for reducing your lot to the size of a drawing board so that you can see it all at once. It is the same as hovering over it in a helicopter, getting a direct vertical view. However, it is even better than this, because with some cheap tracing paper and soft pencils you can plan any number of development schemes complete on the drawing board. This costs no more than the materials and time, and involves no more exertion than the drawing—and the visualizing of what the lines mean at full size on the ground. This last is tough for some of us, as we have mentioned earlier. It is one of those things one learns by doing. The technique of drawing to scale is one all of us should acquire, because sooner or later all of us are apt to get involved in planning some parts of our homes, if not the whole house and lot. Even a cabinet comes out better if drawn to scale first.

Scale means that each inch on the drawing equals a certain number of feet on the ground. This is usually 4, 8, or 16 ft. in garden plan work, depending on the size of the area being shown. A plan is a horizontal section, or slice, through the air above the lot. Everything existing or proposed on the lot is reflected vertically on this horizontal plane, as though it were a piece of glass or sensitized paper. The distance of this horizontal section above the highest point of the lot can be set in order to make the plan clearer. Thus if it is set at 2 ft. above the high ground, it will only show elements BELOW that height. Things above it—such as roofs or tree tops—will be best shown with dotted lines. You have to know where they are, because they affect things placed under them.

SECTIONS AND ISOMETRICS. Once the plan is established you can draw vertical sections or slices, through it. These are taken looking one way or the other, and thus show in their true height and direct elevation all the elements—buildings, trees, shrubs, fences—along that side of the section. This is a technique for finding out the relation between the height of the elements planned and the width of the spaces between them. This helps us to determine whether the garden is getting cluttered with too many

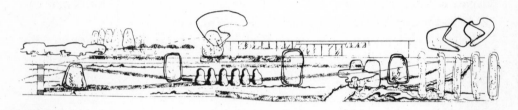

Section

Plan

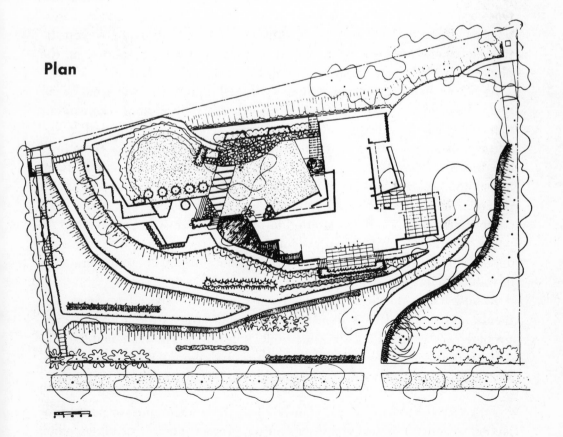

things, whether the elements are the right height, whether the garden may perhaps be too open and simple, and so on.

Another type of drawing which can be projected mechanically from the plan, although it is a little more complicated than direct elevations, is the isometric. This is done by tacking the plan down at an angle on the board, putting a piece of tracing paper over it and drawing in direct elevation at true scale every element on the plan. Those in front will naturally cover some of those in back. When properly set and drawn the isometric gives a very good bird's-eye view of the complete design, and a good opportunity to visualize what it may feel like when and if built. Any good draftsman can show you how plans, sections, and isometrics are drawn.

The first plan made is a survey, which shows the existing condition of the lot as accurately as possible. In addition to structures, trees or other plants, rocks, water, and other elements on the lot, the survey should show the form of the ground accurately.

Elevation differences between various points on the lot (all land slopes some, even if it looks level; you can't trust your eye to determine slopes) are measured with a level on a tripod, and a vertical measure called a rod. One corner of the lot, or some point in it, is taken as 0 or 100, and all elevations measured up or down from it. Professional surveyors may give you the true elevation above sea level instead. These elevations are spotted on the plan, and from the printed spots contour lines can be projected.

A contour line is a dead level line—every point on it is at the same elevation. Therefore it is like a horizontal slice through the ground—the contour marks the line where ground and air meet. The contour interval is the vertical distance between contour lines—usually 1, 2, or 5 ft. Once these lines are drawn on the plan, one can tell what slope exists between any of them by comparing the horizontal distance on plan with this interval. With practice one can learn to read actual ground forms directly and easily from contour drawings. Then new ground forms—earthwork—can be projected on paper by drawing proposed new contour lines. Elevations of true levels—as floors—can be established accurately in relation to these contours, drainage of water can be plotted, and so on.

Details: Once the final plan has been established, special features, elements, and areas within it should be redrawn at larger scale in order to determine exactly how they are to be built or installed. The scale may be 1 or 2 ft. to the inch or even full size at times, and the same pattern of plan, section, or vertical elevation and isometric can be followed.

PLANNING SKILLS. Obviously all of these techniques of paper projection of actual physical conditions on the ground require certain amounts

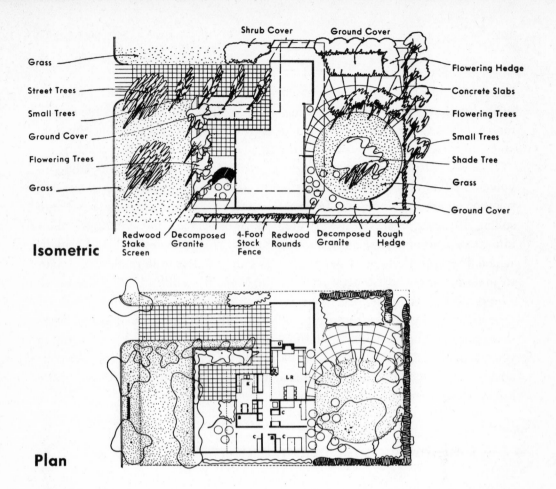

Grass — Street Trees — Small Trees — Ground Cover — Flowering Trees — Grass —

Shrub Cover — Ground Cover

Flowering Hedge — Concrete Slabs — Flowering Trees — Small Trees — Shade Tree — Grass — Ground Cover

Isometric

Redwood Stake Screen | Decomposed Granite | 4-Foot Stock Fence | Redwood Rounds | Decomposed Granite | Rough Hedge

Plan

of skill and practice. The writer is convinced that they should be taught to all of us at the primary or secondary school level, because they constitute a simple common language with which our general problems of shelter and land use can be discussed. There is no other way in which these can be discussed accurately—words are no substitute for drawings. Most American homes would be planned and built much better than they are if their occupants could read blueprints well enough to pick out flaws and omissions, and ask intelligent questions. These techniques can be acquired, in at least their most primitive form, through all sorts of night schools, correspondence courses, or books. If you have not yet acquired them, it would be well worth your trouble to do so now.

Plans are made by all sorts of people—professionals, commercials, amateurs. One of the things which determines their status is their skill at drawing and reading plans and other drawings. A professional is trained in these skills, makes his living by using them daily, and should be able to make and read scale drawings, and semi-scale sketches, better than any nonprofessional. An amateur is anyone without this complete training and experience. He may know almost as much as a professional, nothing at all, or anything in between. His skills are not developed or maintained because he doesn't make his living with them from day to day. It is constant practice which makes perfect—provided the practice is guided by discipline, imagination, and a consistent search for improvement.

Commercial plan-makers do them in order to sell material and labor involved in their execution—plants, fences, barbecues, sprinklers, swimming pools or whatever. They may be professionals or amateurs before they begin selling these things. Whatever their skills may be, and whatever their intentions, these special interests tend to distort and oversimplify the plans which they produce. It is generally difficult for a commercial plan-maker to maintain the consistent search for an over-all solution, using any or all elements other than his. It is this concentration on the best solution, without preconceptions or special interests, which typifies good professional *or* amateur plan-making. Design, including planning, is a special process, not a special person. It requires the development of certain skills and attitudes, combining practicality and imagination. Most of all it requires an open-minded, objective, unprejudiced approach to the problem.

Construction and Installation

Third, once the plans and detailed drawings are completed, construction or installation can begin. Bids or estimates of cost must be secured, so that certain details, such as financing, may be worked out. The purpose of the drawings is to guide and control this operation so that everything comes out as planned. If they are accurate and complete, and if the work is given to a contractor who is competent and honest, there is no reason why this should not happen. However, if there should be some inadequacy in drawings or contractor, then careful supervision, by owner or designer, will be necessary to insure the success of the job. Many designers feel that it is better not to make drawings too complete, as opportunities for improvement of the job, which could not be visualized on paper, may well arise during the course of the work. It is usually possible, with ordinary lot conditions, to design a garden completely and successfully on paper. However, special conditions, problems, or the desire for an exceptional design job may well require a more complete balance between plan design and supervision on the ground. Even professionals feel that solutions are never perfect, improvements are always possible, and one can never tell when inspiration will strike. This does not mean that each of us does not do the best job possible in every working moment.

Plan interpretation. The basic function of supervision is to guarantee proper interpretation of the drawings on the ground, and to make adjustments necessitated by unforeseen circumstances or changes. Particularly with smaller jobs one may very likely find it necessary to work with contractors or craftsmen who are quite competent, but unable to read drawings. Even if they do not admit it, the supervisor must find this out, and provide adequate interpretation of the drawings as the situation may require. All the questions and problems of technique and practical know-how, and of the competence and interest of local labor and craftsmen, come into this construction-installation stage. The drawings may be too complete for the local men to follow, or they may project skills which do not exist locally. On the other hand they may fail to make use of special skills or materials which do exist locally. There are certain problems of detail and practical job procedure which are better solved by the man on the job than by the drawings.

DELEGATION OF WORK. There are three basic methods of executing the plan:

1. A general landscape contractor may be given responsibility for the entire job, including both construction and planting. This is the simplest and least troublesome procedure for the owner, if he does not mind paying the extra profit which the contractor will charge for organizing the various portions of the work. However, an average small landscape job, costing perhaps $2,000, may include earthwork, concrete, wood construction, sprinkler work, planting, and even some other skills. It takes an exceptional contractor to co-ordinate these on small jobs. He may be difficult or impossible to find in your locality.

2. You may therefore find it necessary to let out the various portions of the work separately, either to subcontractors who will supply materials and labor, or by buying the materials yourself and hiring the labor. The skills listed above are typical of the way in which your job may break down. This procedure, while requiring more time and attention from you, will save you some money, and will give you more flexibility in the speed with which the job is finished—and paid for.

3. If your budget proves inadequate for the plan you feel you need—or if you enjoy the work and have time to do it—you can buy the materials and do the installation yourself. This method requires you to develop certain skills if you do not already have them. Each of us must determine which portions of the work we can perform reasonably well ourselves, and which portions should be done by others. But remember that it is better to leave something out than to do it so badly that it will spoil the rest of the garden.

Management

Finally, management (a housewife is a manager) takes over and directs the use and maintenance of the house and garden from then on. Bear in mind that the success of planted landscapes, more than any other type of physical development, is dependent on maintenance. Good care will bring a well-planned garden to successful maturity; bad or inadequate care is apt to destory the quality intended in the plan. On the other hand, many a new dream home has turned out to be an enslaver of the family, presenting them each week end with enough projects to take up all their spare time and energy. For this reason alone the potential maintenance of both construction and planting should be a careful part of the design analysis when the plan is made.

Each of these four steps—program, plan, installation, and maintenance—is of nearly equal importance to the final success of your home project, and it is a practical impossibility to separate one from another, or to eliminate any one. For instance, if a program is not written at the beginning, the designer has to write it as he proceeds with his work, and if he fails to achieve a clear understanding of the problem, the manager (you) may very likely have to write a program for the problem which is supposed to have been solved.

THE BUDGET. The financial problem runs like a strong thread (preferably black) through all of these stages. Part of your program is the establishment of a budget, the amount of money you will be able to, or feel you should, spend on the new development. This has to be set in terms of the rest of the program, that is, what you hope to achieve. This means that if you set your sights too low, if the program is inadequate, then the final result may not be worth the trouble. It is better to shoot for the best and most complete solution, even if it may mean spacing out the actual installation over a period of months or years. Or, if you can afford a good development but don't think the value of the property justifies it ("I'll never get out what I've put into this place"), just remember that any investment which improves your standard of living for a reasonable length of time is worth while for that alone. A good rule of thumb is to expect to spend at least 10 per cent of the lot and house construction cost on the development of the garden.

The budget must also recognize the relation between cost of installation and cost of maintenance. In gardens as in houses, the cheap installation is usually expensive to maintain—in labor if not in money. Conversely, extra money spent for better construction or installation will be saved in reduced maintenance in a short period of time. The cheap house will eat up its savings in painting and patching and repairs in a few years. The cheap planting job will eat up its savings in water and fertilizer and mowing. Extra money spent on soil conditioning will pay off in reduced gardening. Or, spent for paving or construction, it can eliminate some or most of the gardening altogether.

The tragedy in this picture occurs, of course, when the budget is so low in relation to the demands of the program that the problem can only be solved with the cheapest kind of job. This is the tragedy of millions of American families who have moved into cheap jerry-built tract housing in search of their postwar dream home. The burden of maintenance and additional development they have shouldered in order to make and keep the place livable would be staggering if put into true cost figures.

12. At Home in the Neighborhood

Mr. Newfield and Mr. Overbee were talking over the back fence. It was two years since their brave ventures into complete home planning, and the places were beginning to grow up. Mr. Newfield stood halfway above the 6-ft. fence on a stepladder, with a pair of long pruning shears in his hand. His voice was half friendly and half serious.

"You know, Henry," he said, "I'm going to have to start trimming your elm tree. It's shading our roses so much that they're full of mildew, and the flowers are all spoiled."

"Gosh George, that's a real blow. That tree is very important to our bedroom view. Trimming will ruin it."

"But my wife loves roses, and there's no other place in the garden for them. She says I have got to do something about this tree."

"I know you've mentioned this a couple of times before, George. But I just haven't been able to figure out what to do about it. This is one problem we didn't think of when we did all our planning a couple of years ago. Are you sure the roses couldn't go somewhere else in the yard?"

"Henry, we've thought and thought; there's nowhere else to put them." Mr. Newfield's voice was becoming a little strained. "I'm afraid this tree will have to give a little. You know I'm within my legal rights to trim off any parts that hang over the property line."

It was Mr. Overbee's turn to tighten up a little. "But, George, don't you enjoy the form of this tree too? I don't see how you can spoil such a fine specimen just for a few roses. . . ."

Abruptly Mr. Newfield climbed down the stepladder and disappeared. Mr. Overbee heard him stomp into the house and fling down the shears with a

Farm Security Administration

Max Yavno

What is a Neighborhood?

Max Yavno

clatter. Overbee looked unhappily at his tree, then turned wearily toward his own house. It looked like the end of a beautiful friendship. . . .

Mr. Newfield and Mr. Overbee have found out that it is not enough to plan your own yard, no matter how carefully. Unless some minimum cooperation between neighbors exists—so that each neighbor thinks about what his planning may do to the people next door, and knows that they are just as concerned with what they may do to him—problems like the elm and the roses are bound to arise. Sometimes these problems are much worse, as on hillsides where each neighbors' grading and drainage arrangements have a drastic effect on those below him.

Neighbors Must Co-operate

In new tract housing people learn about these problems quite abruptly as soon as they move into the shiny new houses with the raw and empty yards all around them. In solving the first problem—enclosing the yards for control of children, animals and privacy—they find that each fence affects two or more families both economically and visually. Neighborhood social patterns begin their development quite often in new tracts around this question of what kind of fence to build, and who is going to pay for it. Our ideas of free-form fences inside the lot lines will not work in neighborhoods where the people cannot afford to build two fences where one will do the job. Of course with maximum co-operation people might adjust their lot lines in practice on the ground, so as to give each house the best outdoor living space irrespective of legal property lines. However, the bogey of resale would always hang over such informal arrangements.

WHAT IS A NEIGHBORHOOD? What about your neighborhood? Is it pleasant? Do you like most of your neighbors? Are their houses and gardens better, worse or about the same as yours? Does it feel like a real neighborhood? Do you feel that your home is part of it, independent of it, or opposed to it? Do you have a nice home because of the neighborhood, or in spite of it? Where is your school? Where do your children play? Where does your wife shop? Where does your husband meet his friends? Where do you find recreation? What is a neighborhood?

By neighborhood we mean a number of homes grouped together in an area, or a section of a larger community, and using together some or all of the facilities mentioned above. As a result of living together around some community institution—such as a school, a church, a park, or a shopping center—people come to speak of themselves as belonging to the same neighborhood. This is a natural unit of 1,000 to 1,500 families, whose needs can be understood by the people who live in it because they know what they want.

How Neighborhoods Grow. Many very convincing and intriguing plans for such neighborhood prototypes have been developed on paper, and some few—Radburn, N. J.; the Greenbelt towns; various public housing projects; Baldwin Village, Calif.—have been built. Actually most neighborhoods are much more variable as to definition, and, of course, more amorphous as to identity. They constitute some sort of relation between an accumulation of private living space, and the facilities—publicly or privately owned—which are used in common by the residents of that space. Thus a neighborhood as we know it is merely the sum of a number of houses, lots, blocks, and streets, plus whatever common facilities—school, grocery store, drug store, playground—happen to give it some sort of identifying focus or foci. Accidents of planning, of topography, or of traffic may serve to give a few neighborhoods some sense of unity and coherence; beyond these most overlap and run into each other in a most drably indistinguishable fashion.

Mass Production Neighborhoods. New mass-production neighborhoods do little to improve this sterile pattern. In fact most of them are thoroughly regimented, monotonously mediocre, incredibly dull, lacking any semblance of that continuously varying individuality which gives old neighborhoods, however blighted, their warmth and vitality. Nor do these "planned communities" often offer much in the way of community facilities, or public open space, to offset their monotony.

NEIGHBORHOOD TYPES. The variability of the neighborhood concept appears in its relation to varying topography, and to urban, suburban, rural, and even primeval contexts. We think of the urban neighborhood in terms of a range from multi-story apartments to row-houses, and of suburban ranging from two-story apartments to single-family homes. In the rural areas a neighborhood may be a village, or a group of farms scattered over hundreds or thousands of acres, linked primarily by the school bus and the Saturday shopping tour. In primeval areas a neighborhood may be a resort town, or a lumbering or mining or fishing village. But these all present comparable planning problems. The human needs don't change as much as the density imposed by varying community relations. Farmers need social contacts for themselves and their families. City folk need open space and fresh air. Each needs what the other has.

Poverty of Design. In terms of most common standardizations—the gridiron subdivision (whether straight, curved or irregular) with its cardboard dingbat houses; the FHA "garden apartment" group; the typical public housing project with its partiality toward barracksism and its failure to follow through with the potentials of low land coverage—the neighborhood is one of the simplest and most mechanically approached problems in site design. Any school or college complex, any institutional group, any gathering of public buildings, any industrial plant, receives far more elaborate, intensive, and sensitive design concentration than most home-and-services complexes, especially those for the ordinary two-thirds of the population. In fact it is no exaggeration to say that the pattern of most housing neighborhoods, old and new, is set by a bookkeeping process, part of normal real estate practice. A neighborhood is occasionally the result of a professional job of site planning, when it is developed more or less at once, on one piece of real estate; then the program, which determines the quantitative relation of private to public space, is the primary determinant of its quality.

Neighborhoods are usually not site-planning jobs: they just happen through the various accidents of subdivision, speculative building, business adventure, and school or park department land acquisition programs, even within fairly well established city planning procedures. New redevelopment procedures in several cities may produce some new precedents in unified neighborhood planning.

Public and Private Living

Whatever kind of neighborhood it may be in, every home is a direct physical part of it and cannot be separated from it. Most of the functions and facilities of the home are extended or paralleled in the neighborhood. Public access through the front yard is a direct extension of, and connection with, public streets and walks. General living space in the house is paralleled and extended by all sorts of public and private recreational, cultural and relaxation facilities, both indoors and out. Workspaces in the house are paralleled and extended by restaurants, meal services, laundry and dry cleaners, shopping services, child-care centers, housekeepers and domestic help, and so on. Only the private living space of bedroom and bath has no strict parallel in ordinary neighborhoods, unless they include hotel, motel, or guest house accommodations. Thus the relations between each private home and its neighborhood involve continuous choices between social and private living, sociability and privacy, community services and self-sufficient labor, what portions of life can best be handled individually and what portions can best be handled through some form of co-operation within the community.

Although we are primarily concerned with neighborhoods of single-family houses, in all of our cities there are row-house and apartment neighborhoods in which the public services and facilities are highly developed and very convenient. In fact this is the chief reason, in addition to convenience to work, which most urbanites give for living in the city. Although the detached single-family house and garden by their very nature tend to be more self-sufficient than city houses or apartments, there is no particular reason why services in any neighborhood should not be as developed and almost as convenient as in the city, if the residents want them.

EXTENSION OF THE HOME. The local grocery stores or markets are part of our kitchen in the sense that they supply the food which we prepare in it. The local restaurant parallels our own dining room and kitchen, giving us the choice of eating out when we are tired, rushed, or feeling festive. The local movie, library, or soda fountain parallels our living room, giving us a choice of going out among our neighbors or staying home with TV or a book in our spare time. The local cleaner or laundromat parallels our laundry, giving the housewife a chance to break the routine or reduce the burden of household chores, and perhaps socialize a bit in the process. The local nursery school or child-care center parallels the home nursery and its back yard, giving the preschoolers that incomparable opportunity to learn to live with others while they are young, and taking some of the steady burden off the mother. The local school yard or playground is better than streets, and supplements back yards as an outlet for the energies of school-age children. While home is certainly a better place for teen-agers than pool halls and soda fountains, a well-run neighborhood youth center will make it optional to reduce wear and tear on the home. It will also provide adequate neutral space (taking the burden off one or a few homes) for teen-age social activities.

Recreation. Should swimming pools, game courts, children's play-yards, park space with grass and trees, social rooms and buildings, picnic and barbecue areas, walks, horse and bicycle paths be public (by government or private enterprise), private, or both? Obviously there is no general answer to this. In our democracy this is a question for local option within each community, neighborhood and individual family. However, those facilities which are considered essential should certainly be provided publicly for those citizens who cannot afford to duplicate them for their private use. Where public and private facilities parallel each other, the local resident has the broadest opportunity of all. He can use either, as the spirit may move him, and determine on the basis of experience which is better. Certainly as the quantity and quality of neighborhood services and facilities increase, the burden on the private home decreases and its planning becomes simpler. The development in simplification from isolated farm home to city apartment is evidence

Union Pacific Railroad

Max Yavno

Los Angeles Board of Education

of this. The back yard without children's play space, swimming pool, and badminton court can be a simpler and more pleasant outdoor living room, and it can also be smaller and less care.

The Landscape of the Street

These close relations between the private home and its neighborhood are many-sided and inescapable. For instance, the front yard is the direct physical connection between each private home and its neighborhood. Even though privately owned and individually developed, it is nevertheless part of the over-all street picture, which runs from house front to house front across the street. The landscape is everything seen by an individual from any particular spot, or from any path he may follow. Thus it includes both the public right of way, with its street trees and grass parking strips (if any), and all of the front yards insofar as they can be seen at one time. Furthermore, since we remember the things we have seen, as we travel down a street the continuous picture which it unfolds adds up to a continuous impression in our minds. This may be good or bad; it is one of the main factors which we use in determining whether we like a neighborhood.

PUBLIC PLANNING.   Since the street is one picture which is experienced constantly by all the people who live along it or pass through it, we have the continuous problem of determining how much co-operation or mutual agreement there should be in the design and development of this over-all picture. Attempts at solution appear in such conventions as the planned control of street trees by local governments, setback ordinances and restrictions which control the height of plants or structures in front yards, and the universal acceptance of the great American front lawn. The occasional intransigent who wants to vary the trees, fence, or hedge in the front yard, or plant some ground cover or paving instead of grass, is apt to feel that he is going against neighborhood propriety in doing so. He may be projecting an idea which is better for his lot, and very likely for many others. Nevertheless it is difficult for him to go beyond the conventional and accepted solutions.

The implication of these fragmentary controls which have become accepted, plus the fact that physically the street *is* one picture, is that we might have one co-ordinated and planned design for the entire street, block by block, including both private front yards and the public right-of-way. There are many examples of this (usually very oversimplified) in tract housing and multiple apartment projects of various sorts. There are occasional examples of this happening in ordinary single-family house neighborhoods through active agreement and co-operation among the neighbors.

Individual Freedom. The great fear which this idea is apt to invoke in the breast of the average American is that it may involve placing limitations on his personal freedom of expression. The only answer to this fear is the maintenance of democratic processes, through which no such limitations can be established until the agreement of the majority of those directly affected has been secured. This involves the simplest kind of direct meetings and discussion within blocks and neighborhoods. In general, in order to live in communities and work with other people, we all accept certain limitations on our personal freedom. We obey the laws, we conform with time schedules set by others, and so on.

It is not a question of choosing either planning or individuality. A little planning will generally improve the individuality of each front yard, by giving it a better framework in which to display itself. Try comparing the ordinary block of local stores, where the competition between signs and show windows makes it difficult to see any of them, with a planned shopping center, in which control gives each merchant a balanced display which can be seen. The author has designed landscaping for groups of fifty or more houses, in which he made a conscious effort to bring out the individuality of each home within an orderly pattern. Planning in groups, and individualism, are not incompatible. They actually help each other, if basic democratic processes of full information, open discussion, and majority agreement are maintained.

THE MASTER TREE PLAN. Trees are the primary neighborhood amenity. Mature trees in good locations are priceless assets. This value is often realized only after the trees have been lost through carelessness, thoughtlessness, or even dire necessity. Comparison of any new tract on raw land with an old neighborhood full of well-grown trees is enough to prove this point. Almost every tree, whether in front or back yard, can be seen from more than one home. Therefore it affects the lives of more than one family (as the Newfields and Overbees found). The over-all pattern of trees in a neighborhood of detached houses is the single most important visual element. It can integrate the neighborhood, give it identity and character and a sense of unity. Too often it is haphazard, accidental, confused, spotty, or nonexistent.

It is apt to be difficult for us to visualize what a planned tree pattern might do for an average neighborhood. If we think of setting the houses down in a large developed park, or in a rural area with its patterns of wind-

Photo by Walter Chambers

breaks, hedgerows, and orchards, the possibilities will suggest themselves. The restful beauty of a street lined with fine old elms or oaks is no doubt the best known example. Not the least aspect of this beauty is the wonderful sense of three-dimensional space given by the spread and structure of large trees. A master tree plan, developed by co-operative action among the neighbors, could bring these possibilities to every block of houses.

The Neighborhood Landscape

The problem in every neighborhood is the establishment of the best physical relations between private and public activities and facilities, primarily between houses and streets. This helps to determine the quality of the social relations between neighbors. The physical problem has three parts:

1. *Visual:* How does the neighborhood look?
2. *Functional:* Is the land being used to best advantage for everyone?
3. *Maintenance:* Who takes care of the physical elements to keep them looking and functioning well?

These parts all affect each other.

Securing Privacy. The amount of space on private lots which may be screened from public view for private use varies with individuals, neighborhoods, and regions. Elements which may normally be closed in are patios or outdoor living rooms, service and work yards which may be messy to look at, sleeping porches, and suntraps. Larger elements—lawns, gardens, children's play yards, pools and courts—are of course quite often enclosed or screened in for privacy. This latter type of landscape element, because of questions of initial cost, maintenance, and consistency of use, is quite often provided as a neighborhood facility, through public agencies or a neighborhood association. This can save a good deal of duplication of effort and expense among neighbors.

On rough or sloping land the problem of screening for privacy is complicated by the fact that most properties are over-looked by others above them, and all properties want maximum view out.

Tract Restrictions. The neighborhood landscape is everything seen from the streets or from any one house, regardless of whose property it may be on. Therefore practically all the physical development of every property, except those portions which may be screened from public view, is part of the neighborhood landscape.

All of this has been recognized in the legal language of many sets of tract restrictions. Neighborhood associations have been given such powers as the following: approval of all structures down to poles; control of all planting on private lots within 25 ft. of all boundary lines; and the establishment of assessments to provide such conveniences as statues, fountains, park spaces, playgrounds, game courts, and club houses.

However, this control is not enough (and sometimes too much). The neighborhood landscape is compounded of a multitude of specific decisions. In most neighborhoods, even with restrictions such as above, these are made separately, at different times and places, and with little or no direct reference to one another. Restrictions and covenants are usually negative rather than positive in use. The result is usually a hodge-podge, whether the neighborhood is low income or high income.

The Master Plan

The only way to avoid a hodge-podge—and all the various conflicts of trees and views and fences and hedges and pinks and oranges and clotheslines and incinerators and so on which go with it—is to connect and integrate all the specific decisions as closely as possible. This must be done, not in words, but in drawings which are the language of physical development. Since all lots or building sites may not be developed at once, what you need is a master plan which projects the physical development of the entire neighborhood as specifically as possible without inhibiting present or future home owners. This plan should be maintained in a state of flexible development by coordinating it closely with detailed plans for each lot or building site, whether or not they are prepared by the same people. This master plan can project the following:

1. *Land Use and Circulation Pattern.* A detailed projection of relations between houses and other buildings, streets, topography, pedestrian circulation, and various private, semiprivate and public outdoor uses.

2. *Neighborhood Tree Pattern.* This is the basic, three-dimensional spatial structure of the neighborhood, integrating and expressing all the relations between topography, structures, views, open space, and circulation. All of the trees on every lot, as well as those on streets or public spaces, affect all of the neighbors. It is possible with careful planning, based on the needs and desires of all the neighbors, to produce neighborhood patterns of trees more satisfying and beautiful than any known examples. This does not necessarily mean a lot of trees—just the right amount to solve the specific problems of sun and wind and views and desires.

3. *Enclosure Pattern.* Co-ordinating detailed design of fences, walls, gates, and similar structures and all types of boundary plantings—small trees, shrubs, ground covers—in order to produce a detailed harmony at eye level throughout the neighborhood.

4. *Detailed Development.* Detailed development of specific community spaces or facilities which might grow out of the detailed land use and topography analysis, as discussed below.

5. *Engineering.* Coordination of necessary engineering, such as drainage, utilities, and streets, with these elements. There are many gaps between the engineering within public rights-of-way and that on private land.

The essence of the creative potential of the master plan is its co-ordinated projection of all such neighborhood patterns closely integrated with the private plans for each lot or site. In 1944 Revere Copper and Brass Inc. published an intelligent and farsighted little book titled YOU AND YOUR NEIGH-BORHOOD. It was prepared by Oscar Stonorov and Louis I. Kahn, architects, of Philadelphia. The following is quoted or paraphrased from this booklet because it is now out of print. It outlines the basic objectives of neighborhood planning, and the means for achieving them:

MINIMUM REQUIREMENTS. Planners believe a good neighborhood should have: safe streets, a modern school, playgrounds, a neighborhood house, a nursery, a teen-age building, shopping centers, a health center. All these elements that make and serve a neighborhood must be closely related to each other. A large park 5 miles away is no good to the neighborhood—it should be close by. A baseball field 20 blocks away is no good to the neighborhood—it should be close by. A shopping center 10 blocks away is good for the next neighborhood—it should be close by.

THE CITIZEN'S ROLE. Your city or county has all the public agencies that could provide for the needs of the people. However, the planning of your neighborhood to fill these needs is a job *you* have to start. Alone you are powerless. As an individual your power lies in citizen organization. Neighborhoods must re-create the spirit of the New England town meeting to obtain citizen participation, and citizen support for action. Organize a neighborhood planning council. Talk it over with your friends and neighbors. There are undoubtedly civic organizations in your town, neighborhood, or section which are interested in some form of civic advancement. Call a meeting of all those interested: businessmen's organizations, labor unions, professionals, social workers, real estate brokers, ministers, women's clubs. Create block chairmen in each block of your neighborhood to aid the council and divide the work of securing detailed information. A good executive committee might be composed of a businessman, a worker, a housewife, a teacher, a minister, and an engineer, architect, or draftsman (you need somebody on your committee with technical skill who can draw and explain maps). Assemble through your block chairmen a factual recording of the use and conditions of the land of the neighborhood. Evaluate all of this carefully in the council, and decide approximately what steps are needed to improve things. Thereafter, depending upon what sort of community your neighborhood is in, you may contact your city planning department, or other appropriate municipal or county agency, or you may have to go on under the power of your own organization. But improvement is always possible. Where there's a will there's a way.

In Conclusion

We have discussed in considerable detail what landscape problems really are. We have discussed in great detail the procedures, ways and means for improving and solving them through organizing surfacing, enclosure, sheltering, and enriching materials around the central idea of good space for living. We have suggested in sketchy fashion the fact that these landscape problems are shared by us with all our neighbors, that our home does not exist in a physical vacuum. If this discussion proves helpful to you in improving the landscape in which you live, all the effort that went into it will have been well worth while.

Ernest Braun

American Public Health Association, Committee on Hygiene of Housing. *Planning the Neighborhood*. Chicago: Public Administration Service, 1948.

Aronin, Jeffrey. *Climate and Architecture*. New York: Reinhold Pub. Corp, 1953.

Bailey, Liberty H. *Hortus*. New York: Macmillan Co., 1941.

—*Cyclopedia of Horticulture*. New York: Macmillan Co., 1930.

Blumenstock, David I., and Thornthwaite, C. Warren. "Climate and the World Pattern," in *Climate and Man*, 1941 Yearbook of Agriculture. Washington: U. S. Government Printing Office, 1941.

Braun-Blanquet, Josias. *Plant Sociology*. New York: McGraw Hill Book Co., 1932.

Byne, Mildred Stapley, and Byne, Arthur. *Spanish Gardens and Patios*. Philadelphia: J. B. Lippincott Co., 1924.

Census Bureau, U.S. Department of Commerce. *U.S. Statistical Abstract*. Washington: U.S. Government Printing Office; issued annually.

Church, Thomas D. *Gardens Are for People*. New York: Reinhold Pub. Corp., 1955.

Dudley, Leavitt. "When You Shop for Land, You Also Shop for Microclimate," *House Beautiful*, XCVI (May 1954), 180-83.

Eckbo, Garrett. "Small Gardens in the City," *Pencil Points*, XVIII (September 1937), 573-75.

—"Sculpture and Landscape Design," *Magazine of Art*, XXXI (April 1938), 202-08.

—"Progress in Garden Design," in *Gardens and Gardening*, 1939 Studio Annual. London: The Studio Ltd., 1939.

—"Landscaping for Use," *Sunset Magazine*, LXXXV (July 1940), 14-15.

—"Site Planning," *Architectural Forum*, LXXVI (May 1942), 263-65.

—"Landscape Gardening I: The Small Lot," *Architectural Forum*, LXXXIV (February 1946), 76-80.

—"Landscape Gardening II: Community Planning," *Architectural Forum*, LXXXIV (March 1946), 141-44.

—"What Is Landscape Architecture?" *Arts and Architecture*, LXII (October 1945), 40-41.

Emerson, Fred. *Basic Botany*. Philadelphia: Blakiston Co., 1947.

Fitch, James Marsten. *American Building*. Boston: Houghton Mifflin Co., 1948.

French, Leigh, and Eberlein, Harold Donaldson. *The Smaller Houses and Garden of Versailles*. New York: Reinhold Pub. Corp., 1926.

Gallotti, Jean. *Moorish Houses and Gardens of Morocco*. New York: William Helburn Inc., 1926.

Gardner, Victor Ray. *Basic Horticulture*. New York: Macmillan Co., 1951.

Gothein, Marie Louise. *A History of Garden Art*. New York: E. P. Dutton & Co., 1928.

Graham, Dorothy. *Chinese Gardens*. New York: Dodd, Mead & Co., 1938.

Greenough, Horatio. *Form and Function*. Berkeley and Los Angeles: University of California Press, 1947.

Gutheim, Frederick. *Houses for Family Living*. New York: Woman's Foundation, Inc., 1948.

Hamblin, Stephen F. *List of Plant Types*. Cambridge: Harvard University Press, 1929.

Hamlin, Talbot. *Architecture Thtough the Ages*. New York: G. P. Putnam's Sons, 1940.

Harwood, W. S. *Luther Burbank and New Creations in Plant Life*. New York: Macmillan Co., 1906.

Hitchcock, Henry-Russell. *In the Nature of Materials: The Buildings of Frank Lloyd Wright*. New York: Duell, Sloan & Pearce, 1942.

Hoyt, R. S. *Ornamental Plants for Subtropical Regions*. Los Angeles: Livingston Press, 1938.

Hudnut, Joseph. "Space in the Modern Garden," *Bulletin of the Garden Clubs of America* VII (May 1946), 16-24.

Imlay, Catherine. "Reid Garden: 'Landplanning' Knits House and Site Together," *Sunset Magazine,* XCVI (May 1946), 20-23.

Kellogg, Charles E. "Climate and Soil," in *Climate and Man,* 1941 Yearbook of Agriculture. Washington: U. S. Government Printing Office, 1941.

—*The Soils That Support Us.* New York: Macmillan Co., 1941.

Kennedy, Robert Woods. *The House.* New York: Reinhold Pub. Corp., 1953.

Kepes, Gyorgy. *The Language of Vision.* Chicago: Paul Theobald, 1944.

Kuck, Lorraine E. *The Art of Japanese Gardens.* New York: John Day, 1940.

—*One Hundred Kyoto Gardens.* London: Kegan Pau, Trench, Trubner & Co., 1935.

Le Corbusier. *Towards A New Architecture.* New York: Payson & Clarke Ltd., 1927.

Lobeck, Armin Kohl. *Geomorphology.* New York: McGraw-Hill Book Co., 1939.

Lord, Russell. *To Hold This Soil.* (U.S. Soil Conservation Service). Washington: U.S. Government Printing Office, 1938.

Moholy-Nagy, Ladislaus. *Vision in Motion.* Chicago: Paul Theobald, 1947.

Nichols, Rose Standish. *Spanish and Portuguese Gardens.* Boston: Houghton Mifflin Co., 1924.

Peattie, Donald Culross. *Flowering Earth.* New York: G. P. Putnam's Sons, 1939.

Person, H. S. *Little Waters.* (U.S. Soil Conservation Service). Washington: U.S. Government Printing Office, 1936.

Platt, Rutherford. *Our Flowering World.* New York: Dodd, Mead & Co., 1947.

Pope, Arthur Upham. "Persian Gardens: Formative Factors in Persian Art," in *Introduction to Persian Art Since the Seventh Century A.D.* London: P. Davies, 1930.

Raunkiaer, Christen. *Life Forms of Plants.* Oxford: Clarendon Press, 1934.

Robbins, W. W., and Weier, T. E. *Botany, An Introduction to Plant Science.* New York: John Wiley & Sons, 1950.

Rose, James C. "Freedom in the Garden," *Pencil Points,* XIX (October 1938), 639-43.

—"Plants Dictate Garden Forms," *Pencil Points,* XIX (November 1938), 695-97.

—"Integration," *Pencil Points,* XIX (December 1938), 758-60.

—"Articulate Form in Design," *Pencil Points,* XX (February 1939), 98-100.

—"Plant Forms and Space," *Pencil Points,* XX (April 1939), 227-28.

—"Why Not Try Science?" *Pencil Points,* XX (December 1939), 777-79.

Rose, James C., Kiley, Daniel U., and Eckbo, Garrett. "Landscape Design in the Urban Environment," *Architectural Record,* LXXXV (May 1939), 70-77.

—"Landscape Design in the Rural Environment," *Architectural Record,* LXXXVI (August 1939), 68-74.

—"Landscape Design in the Primeval Enronment," *Architectural Record,* LXXXVII (February 1940), 74-79.

Sale, Edith Tunis. *Historical Gardens of Virginia.* (James River Garden Club). Richmond: William Byrd Press, 1923.

San Francisco Museum of Art and American Association of Landscape Architects. *Landscape Design, San Francisco Bay Region.* San Francisco: San Francisco Museum of Art, 1948.

Shepherd, J. C., and Jellicoe, G. A. *Italian Gardens of the Renaissance.* New York: Charles Scribner's Sons, 1925.

Shiga, Nayoya, and Motoi, Hashimoto, Editors. *Gardens of Japan.* Tokyo: The Zauho Press, 1935.

Shuler, Ellis W. *Rocks and Rivers.* Lancaster, Pa.: Jacques Cattell Press, 1945.

Sirén, Osvald. *Gardens of China.* New York: Ronald Press, 1949.

Stonorov, Oscar, and Kahn, Louis I. *You and Your Neighborhood.* New York: Revere Copper and Brass Inc., 1944.

Studio Annual. *Gardens and Gardening.* London: The Studio Ltd.; issued annually.

Sullivan, Louis. *Autobiography of an Idea.* Washington: American Institute of Architects, 1924. New York: Peter Smith, 1949.

—*Kindergarten Chats.* New York: Wittenborn, Schultz, Inc., 1947.

Sunset Magazine. *Sunset Western Garden Book.* Menlo Park, California: Lane Publishing Co., 1954.

Tamura, Tsuyoshi. *Art of the Landscape Garden in Japan.* Tokyo: Kokusai Bunka Shinkokai, 1936.

Tunnard, Christopher. *Gardens in the Modern Landscape.* New York: Charles Scribner's Sons, 1948.

U.S. Department of Agriculture. *Soils and Man,* 1938 Yearbook of Agriculture. Washington: U.S. Government Printing Office, 1938.

U.S. Soil Conservation Service. Soil conservation publications. Washington: U.S. Government Printing Office.

Van Dyke, John C. *Nature for Its Own Sake.* New York: Charles Scribner's Sons, 1921.

Villiers Stuart, C. M. *Gardens of the Great Mughals.* London: Adam and Charles Black, 1913.

Visher, Stephen Sargent. *Climatic Atlas of the United States.* Cambridge: Harvard University Press, 1954.

Weaver, John E., and Clements, Frederic E. *Plant Ecology.* New York: McGraw-Hill Book Co., 1929.

Weir, Wilbert W. *Soil Science.* Chicago and Philadelphia: J. B. Lippincott Co., 1936.

Whiting, John R. *A Treasury of American Gardening.* New York: Doubleday & Co., 1954.

Whitson, John; Williams, Robert John; and Williams, Henry Smith. *Luther Burbank.* New York and London: L. B. Press, 1914.

Wilenski, R. H. *The Meaning of Modern Sculpture.* New York: Frederick A. Stokes Co., 1935.

Wright. Richardson. *The Story of Gardening.* New York: Garden City Publishing Co., 1938.

Wyman, Donald. *Shrubs and Vines in American Gardens.* New York: Macmillan Co., 1949.

—*Trees for American Gardens.* New York: Macmillan Co., 1951.

INDEX

Abstraction or representation, 214, 218
Acoustics, 207 f.
Adobe as paving material, 129
Alpines, 190, 200
Amateur or professional design, 65, 251 ff.
Angle of repose, 114, 136, 164
Angles in garden design, 67
Animals in landscape, 200, 202
Annual beds, 186 ff.
Annuals and perennials, maintenance of, 242
Aquatics, 189, 192
Arc-and-tangent, 67
Architect, retention of, 11
Architectural decoration, 215
Architectural enclosure, 163
Architectural forms, 66
Architecture, contemporary residential, 185
Arrangement of plants, 163, 238
Art elements, 71, 213 ff.
  forms, 186, 215 f., 218
  objects, 186
  principles, 71

Balance in design, 74
Barbecues, cautions concerning, 208
  as enrichment elements, 186
Bedrock, relation to grading, 119
Beds, cultivated, 136, 141, 186 ff.
Berms, protective, 114
Biennials, characteristics of, 190
Bitumils, for hard paving, 130
Bog gardens, 189 f.
  plants for, 192
Botanical names, significance of, 224
Botany, branches of, 222
Boulders as sculpture, 160
Brazier for barbecue, 208
Brick, as paving material, 129
  for walls, 157
Brick, crushed, as special aggregate, 130
Budget coordinated with plan, 167, 254
Building codes, for garden enclosures, 166
  for garden shelters, 170 f.
Bulkheads for steep slopes, 137

Cacti, 189, 190 ff.
Cantilever, for difficult slopes, 139
  for masonry walls, 157
Catch basins for terraces, 120
Ceramics, for enrichment, 186, 218
Changes in level, 136 f.
  see also Grading
Children, neighborhood facilities for, 262
Chinese gardens, nonlinear pattern in, 70
  rock work in, 160
Circular forms, 67
Circulation patterns, in the home, 48
  in the neighborhood, 269

Clay products, in masonry, 157 f.
Climate, control of, 45 f., 171
  and flower gardening, 189
  and people, 18
  regional classification, 21 f.
Codes and permits, 166, 170
Color, in paints and stains, 186, 211 ff.
  in plants, 233, 235
Community, development of, 270
  planning for, 265
Compaction of soil, 116, 118 f.
Competition among plants, 222
Composting, 123, 125
Concrete, for hard paving, 129 f.
Concrete blocks, for enclosure, 158
Construction, and installation, 252 f.
  masonry, 157 f.
  rock, 158 f.
  wood, 154
Containers for water, 164, 196
Contour lines, plotting, 250
Cooperation among neighbors, 259
Costs, budgeting of, 167
  labor, 253
Cribbing for steep slopes, 114, 139
Crushed material for surfacing, 130
Cultivation of planting, 136

Design, balance in, 74
  of garden enclosure, 143
  in ground cover, 135
  principles, 54 ff.
  process, 71, 252
  professional or amateur, 251
  vocabulary, 65-70
Ditches, drainage, 114
Drainage, 113 ff.
  controls, 116, 119 ff., 123
  fast, 121
  on sloping ground, 24, 139
  slow, 121
  subsurface, 119
  surface, 119
Drawings; see Plans
Driftwood, as enrichment, 186, 194
Dry walls, planting for, 190
  for steeper slopes, 137

Earth, as enclosure, 164
  see also Soils
Earthwork, budget for, 253
  techniques, 114
Ecology, maintenance and, 239
  science of, 222, 224
Elements, control of, 182 f.
  Emphasis in design, 74